VANDANA SHIVA is a world-renowned environmental thinker and activist, a leader in the International Forum on Globalisation, and of the Slow Food Movement. Director of Navdanya and of the Research Foundation for Science, Technology and Ecology, and a tireless crusader for farmers', peasants' and women's rights, she is the author and editor of a score of influential books, among them *Making Peace with the Earth*; *Soil Not Oil*; *Globalization's New Wars*; *Seed Sovereignty, Food Security: Women in the Vanguard*; and *Who Really Feeds the World?*

Shiva is the recipient of over twenty international awards, including the Right Livelihood Award (1993); Medal of the Presidency of the Italian Republic (1998); the Horizon 3000 Award (Austria, 2001); the John Lennon-Yoko Ono Grant for Peace (2008); the Save the World Award (2009); the Sydney Peace Prize (2010); the Calgary Peace Prize (2011); and the Thomas Merton Award (2011). She was the Fukuoka Grand Prize Laureate in 2012.

KARTIKEY SHIVA is a shatterer of illusions, grower of freedom, and agent of light.

All of us who care about the future of Planet Earth must be grateful to Vandana Shiva. Her voice is powerful, and she is not afraid to tackle those corporate giants that are polluting, degrading and ultimately destroying the natural world.
—Jane Goodall, UN Messenger of Peace

Her fierce intellect and her disarmingly friendly, accessible manner have made her a valuable advocate for people all over the developing world.
—Ms. magazine

A rock star in the worldwide battle against genetically modified seeds.
—Bill Moyers

Shiva is a burst of creative energy, an intellectual power.
—The Progressive

One of the world's most prominent radical scientists.
—The Guardian

ALSO BY VANDANA SHIVA

Who Really Feeds the World? (2016)

Seed Sovereignty, Food Security: Women in the Vanguard (2015)

Making Peace with the Earth: Beyond Resource, Land and Food Wars (2012)

Soil Not Oil: Climate Change, Peak Oil and Food Insecurity (2009)

Globalization's New Wars: Seed, Water & Life Forms (2005)

Water Wars: Privatization, Pollution and Profit (2002)

Stolen Harvest: The Hijacking of the Global Food Supply (2000)

Biopiracy: The Plunder of Nature and Knowledge (1997)

Ecofeminism (co-authored with Maria Mies, 1993)

Monocultures of the Mind: Biodiversity, Biotechnology and Agriculture (1993)

The Violence of the Green Revolution: Ecological Degradation and Political Conflict in Punjab (1992)

Staying Alive: Women, Ecology and Survival in India (1988, 2010)

ONENESS VS. THE 1%

SHATTERING ILLUSIONS, SEEDING FREEDOM

VANDANA SHIVA
WITH
KARTIKEY SHIVA

Chelsea Green Publishing
White River Junction, Vermont
London, UK

Oneness vs. the 1%: Shattering Illusions, Seeding Freedom was first published in India in
2018 by Women Unlimited (an associate of Kali for Women), 7/10, FF, Sarvapriya
Vihar, New Delhi - 110 016.

This edition published by Chelsea Green Publishing, 2020.

Project Editor: Brianne Goodspeed
Indexer: Nancy Crompton

Printed in the United States of America.
First printing August 2020.
10 9 8 7 6 5 4 3 2 1   20 21 22 23 24

Library of Congress Cataloging-in-Publication Data
Names: Shiva, Vandana, author. | Shiva, Kartikey, author.
Title: Oneness vs. the 1% : shattering illusions, seeding freedom / Vandana
    Shiva, with Kartikey Shiva.
Description: White River Junction, Vermont : Chelsea Green Publishing,
    2020. | First published in 2018 in India. | Includes bibliographical
    references and index.
Identifiers: LCCN 2020029374 (print) | LCCN 2020029375 (ebook) |
    ISBN 9781645020394 (paperback) | ISBN 9781645020400 (ebook) |
    ISBN 9781645020417 (audio)
Subjects: LCSH: Income distribution.
Classification: LCC HC79.I5 S45 2020 (print) | LCC HC79.I5 (ebook) | DDC
    339.2—dc23
LC record available at https://lccn.loc.gov/2020029374
LC ebook record available at https://lccn.loc.gov/2020029375

Chelsea Green Publishing
85 North Main Street, Suite 120
White River Junction, Vermont USA

Somerset House
London, UK

www.chelseagreen.com

Contents

Preface

What is it to live, to be alive? What is it to live well, to be well?
What is knowledge, what is intelligence?
What is ecology, what is economy?
What is freedom, what is democracy?
What is our future?

We are compelled to return to these basic questions in our times—times of the possible extinction of our species, as the current dominant model of knowledge, of 'wealth' creation, and of 'representative' democracy violates planetary boundaries, the rights of the diverse species that share this planet, as well as the human rights and freedoms of most people. Times when the 1% controls the wealth and power to destroy our planet and our common lives, with no responsibility or accountability for their actions, because they have found clever ways to create illusions—of the separation of humans from the earth, and of the 1% from the rest of society, as if we share no common wealth, and no common future.

Being well and the experience of wellbeing are timeless—off the clock. 'Wealth' means a state of wellbeing. The market has come between us and our wellbeing, severing us from our potential and needs. The market has also allowed its own consolidation, accompanied by the consolidation of global power.

In 2010, 388 billionaires controlled as much wealth as the bottom half of humanity; this number came down to 177 in 2011; to 159 in 2012; 92 in 2013; 80 in 2014; and 62 in 2016; it shrivelled to a mere eight in 2017. By 2020, it seems, there will be only ONE.

In 2008, during the global economic crash when people lost their homes and jobs, billionaires consolidated their ownership of industry across the world. Stock prices had bottomed out, and the wealthiest billionaires bought out the economy at bottom-dollar prices. It was too convenient to be a matter of chance—this was the deployment of the money machine.

The money machine is programmed to bulldoze, destroy, aggregate and accumulate, externalise and excavate. Like the cancer cell which does not know when to stop growing, convergences, mergers and concentration are the only logic the money machine understands. And just as the cancer cell ends up destroying the host organism, the money machine, too, will destroy the planet and our societies from which it draws its support.

We must reclaim our intelligence and creativity to resist the money machine and create non-violent alternatives. We must reclaim the market from the money machine, and our lives from billionaire dictators. We must reclaim our real freedoms, and not be seduced by the false freedoms of 'free trade', corporate rule, algorithm-run democracy, and consumerism. We must stand firm and reclaim the meaning of wealth and the conditions for being well.

Will the 'end game' for humanity be the domination of the ONE power of Big Money, or will we, in our Oneness—as one earth community, one human community—shut down the 'Operating System' of domination and extermination, to allow our potential for self-organisation and creativity to seed another future?

Preface

The diversity of cultures and languages, and with them, our imagination, is being lost. Social violence and disintegration have become the norm everywhere, as economic polarisation and inequalities deepen. Every society is facing a crisis of democracy, as Big Money hijacks the process of representative democracy, and elections are used to divide people through hate and fear; they divert the public consciousness from the real roots of their insecurity, thus preventing them from organising and rising to protect the planet, to rebuild their societies, and to reclaim their economies and democracies.

Humanity stands at a precipice. There is an uncertainty regarding our potential for future evolution. Ecologically, the uncertainty arises because every aspect of the dominant model of thinking and living is destroying the earth's capacity to support our lives. The erosion and extinction of our species, the destruction of soils and water, and climate chaos, are wreaking havoc on the conditions necessary to continue as members of the earth community. The extractive model of economic development and growth, of corporate control and the greed economy are not just destroying nature, they are destroying our humanity which is the human capacity for solidarity, compassion, and the ability to take care of each other.

Through the illusions and abstractions that the powerful have created and imposed on the rest of humanity, especially over the last two centuries of the rise of fossil fuel-based industrialism and the mechanical, reductionist mind, we are losing our capacity to not just sustain life ecologically but also to sustain life socially, as a community. Uprooting, dispossession, the creation of refugees, is the shadow of the illusionary model of limitless growth, on a planet with ecological limits, as well as of the exercise of limitless power by the powerful, through constructed grids of categories and narratives.

But going off the precipice, towards extinction, is not inevitable. We can choose to walk away from the mechanistic world of invented constructions, and free ourselves from the forces and paradigms that have brought us to it. We can realise that we are members of the earth community and that the earth has an amazing capacity and potential to rejuvenate and renew; and since we are part of the earth, not separate from her, we share that capacity and potential. A consciousness of our power to 'be the change we want to see', as Gandhi said, forms the basis for cultivating hope, love, and compassion in these times of despair, fear and hate.

Within the crises that have brought us to the precipice lie the seeds of hope and freedom, the seeds to renew our humanity and our earth citizenship. The crisis of survival that we face today is a result of the domination of an extractive economy, imposed by artificial separations constructed by the mechanical mind, and the false assumption that greed is a virtue to be rewarded by society. In an interview in May 2017, Stephen Hawking said that humanity faces a survival crisis... that it is so severe that in the next hundred years, either humanity will be extinct or we will have to escape from the earth and colonise other planets.[1]

This idea of violating planetary limits for the next conquest, the next escape, only furthers the illusionary idea of linear human progress, bereft of oneness with the earth and the recognition that this is our home, the only one we have, and that the crisis we find ourselves in is, in fact, a consequence of the colonisation of the earth, of diverse cultures, and of the absence of accountability for the destruction caused by colonisation. Escape is what led to colonisation in the past—and the same logic of mastery and conquest is being applied now to colonise other planets.

Cecil Rhodes, who colonised Zimbabwe (formerly Rhodesia), stated frankly,

> We must find new lands from which we can easily obtain raw materials and at the same time exploit the cheap slave labour that is available from the natives of the colonies. The colonies would also provide a dumping ground for the surplus goods produced in our factories.[2]

This is what the economy of the 1% is modelled on. The tools of extraction and the colonies might change, but the methods of colonisation remain unchanged—grab and steal what belongs to others, make it your own property, collect rents from the original owners, and convert the displaced into cheap slave labour to provide raw material, as well as to become the market for your industrial products.

This form of colonisation, of nature and people, however, is reaching its limits now. When there is no need for slaves, no need for exploited workers, who will buy the junk that the 1% has to offer—junk food and junk clothing, junk communications and junk media; when the earth is exploited and polluted, rupturing planetary limits; and when her life support systems are destroyed, there will be no production. No survival.

But there are options beyond colonisation, beyond extinction. There is a third option—that of staying alive by caring for the earth and for each other, rejuvenating the planet and our common humanity.

Only as one earth community and one humanity, united in our diversities, can we hold ourselves together, step away from the precipice and escape the destructive, ecocidal, genocidal rule of the 1%. We can turn around and walk to our freedom. To live free. Think free. Breathe free. Eat free.

This book is an expression of hope, rooted in oneness—the philosophy of *vasudhaiva kutumbakam*, one earth family. It is based on the hope that proceeds from our potential to transcend separation and division—to think, act and live as one humanity on one planet with full consciousness of our interconnectedness, as well as our responsibility to participate actively, every day, every moment of our lives, to protect and rejuvenate the natural and social web of life. His Holiness the Karmapa, Ogyen Trinley Dorje, has called it compassionate courage, the courage to act from compassion.[3]

We have created freedom and liberation movements before. We have decolonised our minds and our cultures from the stains and chains of imperialism, and shed the artificially constructed (but 'naturalised') categories of race, gender, class and colour. We can, through our creativity and imagination, through our solidarity and interconnectedness, create a planetary freedom movement through which we break free of the chains and walls constructed by the illusions of the mechanical mind, the money machine and the delusion of democracy. We can reclaim and create real knowledge through real intelligence. We can reclaim and create real wealth with nature, through our creativity. We can sow the seeds of real freedom and earth democracy.

Now has always been our time. This is the Resurgence of the Real. The real is our oneness and non-separability. The real is our lived and living intelligence. The real is our self-organisation, our creativity, our freedom. The real is our potential to sow the seeds of diversity, of hope, of compassion, of interconnectedness, of our common future.

Preface

Endnotes

[1] Chris McDermott, 'Stephen Hawking: We Have 100 Years to Find a New Planet', *EcoWatch*. http://www.ecowatch.com/stephen-hawking-bbc-2392439489.html. Published on May 4, 2017.

[2] Terry Gibbs, *Why the Dalai Lama is a Socialist: Buddhism and the Compassionate Society*. London: Zed Books, 2017, p. 116.

[3] HH The Karmapa, Ogyen Trinley Dorje, *Interconnected: Embracing Life in Our Global Society*. Massachusetts: Wisdom Publications, 2017.

1 1% vs. One Earth, One Humanity

We are one earth family, one humanity
We are connected through our diversity, intelligence, creativity and compassion

FOR the first time in human history, our common future as a species is no longer certain. In just 500 years of colonisation, including 200 years of a fossil fuel age and 20 years of corporate globalisation, humanity has done enough damage to the earth to ensure its own extinction. The blindness of the 1% to the potential of life, to the rights of people, to the destructive impacts of their 'constructs', has ensured that going over the precipice is inevitible. They define their destructive, colonising power as 'superior' while the creative, nonviolent forces of nature, and of women, indigenous people, and farmers, is perceived as 'backwardness' or 'passivity'. In their constructed narrative of linear progress, there is only one way—forward. But when you are already standing at a precipice, going forward means going hurtling down.

Our common and indivisible freedoms, through our diversities, are being threatened by the freedoms that the 1% have created for themselves through free trade agreements, tools of mass manipulation, and the enclosure of the commons through patents. They are consolidating further by enforcing uniformity and monocultures, division and separation, monopolies and external control, centralisation and coercion, and imposing their paradigms and narratives undemocratically on the world. The economically and politically powerful 1%, disconnected from the earth and humanity (including their own), are trying to control every sphere of our lives.

1% vs. One Earth, One Humanity

Diversity and our interconnected freedoms

Oneness is the very source of our existence, our interconnectedness with the universe, with all beings (including human beings), and with our local communities. Oneness is woven through our diverse living intelligence and creativity. It represents the confluence of our rich and vibrant diversities—biodiversity, cultural diversity, economic diversity, political diversity and knowledge diversity. It is based on the deep understanding that life and freedom are one, that our freedom, as humans and as members of the earth community, is not separable from the freedom of the earth. Trees and plants provide human beings with oxygen, and humans and other animals provide the necessary carbon dioxide in the living carbon cycle. Trees create the conditions for our freedom. The mycorrhizal fungi in the soil provide nourishment to plants and derive their own nutrition from them. The freedom of plants is dependent on the freedom of the mycorrhizal fungi. And soil rich in organic matter has abundant beneficial fungi which are useful to plants and, ultimately, to humans and animals who consume them; our freedom to live and thrive are interconnected.

Concern and care for our seeds, our soil, our air, and our water are the real test of our commitment to our future. The processes that are killing our soil, our biodiversity, our air, water and climate balance are also killing our humanity.

Compassion arises naturally, from connectedness and the consciousness of being interconnected. It is not the 'philanthrophy' of billionaires, because their billions are made through the violent economies of extraction, and because they use their billions in philanthropy to create more markets and make more money. Above all, 'philanthropy' is not compassion because it assumes that money is the only human currency. This is an emergency. And yet, our response does not address the root causes of the crises we are facing.

We are at a critical juncture in the evolution of the planet, and in our evolution as a species. More than 90 per cent of crop varieties have disappeared; some 75 per cent of plant genetic diversity has been pushed to extinction by the monocultures of the mechanical mind.[1] We are living in the age of the sixth extinction; this is the moment where we need to rejuvenate biodiversity on our farms and in our fields, in our kitchens and on our plates, to address the climate crisis, the health crisis, the crisis of corporate control over our food.

According to poet and philosopher Rabindranath Tagore, the distinctiveness of Indian culture is in its having defined life in the forest as the highest form of cultural evolution. In his essay, *Tapovan*, he writes,

> Contemporary western civilisation is built of brick and wood. It is rooted in the city. But Indian civilisation has been distinctive in locating its source of regeneration, material and intellectual, in the forest, not the city. India's best ideas have come where man was in communion with trees and rivers and lakes, away from the crowds. The peace of the forest has helped the intellectual evolution of man. The culture of the forest has fuelled the culture of Indian society. The culture that has arisen from the forest has been influenced by the diverse processes of renewal of life which are always at play in the forest, varying from species to species, from season to season, in sight and sound and smell. The unifying principle of life in diversity, of democratic pluralism, thus became the principle of Indian civilisation.

Forests are the storehouse of biodiversity and can teach us

4

lessons in democracy; of sharing space with others while drawing sustenance from the common web of life.

Democracy is participation, and since participation is embodied, not disembodied, participatory democracy is a lived and living democracy. We must build a movement to recognise the Rights of Nature and Mother Earth, and the violations of these rights as ecocide.[2]

Life is self-organised, life is intelligent

Every cell, every microbe, every being is autonomous and autopoietic, self-organised and free, dynamic and evolving, interconnected and non-separable. Scientists Humberto Maturana and Francisco Varela have identified living systems as autopoietic—organised from within.[3] Machines, on the other hand, are allopoietic systems—assembled and controlled externally. One of the most dramatic ontological shifts of our time is redefining living organisms, especially seeds, as machines 'invented' by corporations.

Over two centuries of the fossil fuel-driven industrial age, an intellectual architecture has been created which artificially separates us from the earth, and from each other. I have called it 'eco-apartheid', the imagined separation between humans and nature. Bruno Latour calls it the 'partitioning, or deepening the imaginary gulf between nature and culture'.[4]

In the dominant mechanistic paradigm, not only are humans separated from nature, nature is declared dead inert matter, mere raw material for exploitation. The mechanistic worldview was crafted to serve industrial capitalism which elevated an inadequate, reductionist, mechanistic paradigm to the level of science, while scientific thought, based on the awareness of a living earth, was politically relegated to non-science, even anti-science. Ecological and social ignorance, combined with greed and the urge to dominate and control, has given us the dominant economic, political, scientific, technological systems that the 1% use to rule the world today.

When our age is called Anthropocene, it refers to the power of man to disrupt the earth's ecological processes. It would be arrogant and irresponsible to claim that the power to destroy gives some humans the right to take over the earth's resources, processes and systems. If we are alive today it is because the earth is alive and creates the conditions of our lives. To be alive on this beautiful planet is to live in the Ecocene.

The arrogance of colonialism and industrialism lies in assuming that only the coloniser has intelligence. Whereas real intelligence is signified by evolutionary and ecological intelligence, it has, like everything else, been been reduced to mechanical and analytic intelligence, and is now further outsourced as 'artificial intelligence'. Not only have we reduced our intelligence to just one form, shaped by the mechanical mind, the anthropocentric and mechanistic bias in science has blinded us to the pervasiveness of living intelligence.

English botanist Sir Albert Howard, who came to India in 1905 to introduce western systems of farming, instead found extremely sophisticated systems which had sustained Indian agriculture over the millennia. He decided to make the local peasants and pests his teachers on good farming practices. *The Agriculture Testament* was a synthesis of his learnings, and is now referred to as the bible of modern organic farming. Among the key lessons he learnt were those of diversity and the law of return. Sustainable agriculture is based on diversity—integrating different crops, trees and animals on a farm. Diverse crops produce diverse nutrients for the soil, and for animals as well as humans.

The law of return is based on giving back to nature and society what we receive from them. Howard applied his scientific training to understand the ecology of the soil, based on the practice of the law of return, and evolved the famous method of composting known as the 'Indore method'. The loss of biodiversity in our fields and from our diet, due to the spread of the Green Revolution and industrial agriculture over the last fifty years is not just contributing to an ecological crisis, it is leading to a disease epidemic.

Plants are the very basis of life. The tradition of seeing trees and plants as alive was continued in modern times by the eminent Indian scientist, J.C. Bose, who conducted detailed experiments to show that the impulse of men and animals for undisputed superiority over their hitherto 'vegetative brethren' did not bear the test of close inspection. According to him,

> These experiments bring the plant much closer to humans than we ever thought. We find that it is not a mere mass of vegetative growth, but that its every fibre is instinct with sensibility. We are able to record the throbbing of its pulsating life, and find that these wax and wane according to the life conditions of the plant, and cease in the death of the organism. In these and many other ways, the life reactions in plant and man are alike.[5]

Eating is an act of communication. In eating, we communicate with the earth, the farmer, the chef. Our food communicates with the beneficial bacteria in our gut which enable us to maintain our health and increase our resistence to disease. Our gut is a microbiome which contains 100 trillion microbes and

1,000 bacterial species with more than 7 million genes. For every human gene, there are 360 bacterial genes in our body. Only 10 per cent of the cells in the human body are human. There are 100,000 times more microbes in our gut than people on the planet.

And bacteria are intelligent. James Shapiro has called bacteria sentient beings. According to him,

> … bacteria possess many cognitive, computational and evolutionary capabilities…Studies show that bacteria utilize sophisticated mechanisms for intercellular communication and even have the ability to commandeer the basic cell biology of "higher" plants and animals to meet their basic needs…. This remarkable series of observations requires us to revise basic ideas about biological information processing and recognise that even the smallest cells are sentient beings.[6]

The poisonous pesticides and herbicides we use on our food destroy the beneficial bacteria in our gut, leading to serious diseases, from intestinal disorders to neurological problems such as autism and Alzheimer's. Centers for Disease Control (CDC) data show that on current trends one-in-two children in the US will be found to be autistic in a few decades. It is not an intelligent species that destroys its own future because of a distorted and manipulated definition of science.[7]

As systems thinker Yaneer Bar-Yam has written,

> A complex system is formed out of many components whose behaviour is emergent…the behaviour of the system cannot be simply inferred from the behaviour of its components…emergent properties cannot be studied by physically taking a system apart and looking at the parts (reductionism).[8]

Mechanistic reductionism is based on seeing the world

as a machine, and knowledge based on separation as the only knowledge that counts. Carl Woese called mechanistic reductionism a 'fundamentalist reductionism'. He says,

> We need to distinguish what can be called 'empirical reductionism' from 'fundamentalist reductionism'. Empirical reductionism is in essence methodological; it is simply a mode of analysis, the dissection of a biological entity or system into its constituent parts in order to better understand it. Empirical reductionism makes no assumptions about the fundamental nature, an ultimate understanding, of living things. Fundamentalist reductionism (the reductionism of nineteenth century classical physics), on the other hand, is in essence metaphysical. It is ipso facto a statement about the nature of the world: living systems (like all else) can be completely understood in terms of the properties of their constituent parts.[9]

The knowledge we need for breeding, selecting, evolving seeds and growing food is the knowledge of biodiversity and living seed, of living soil and the soil-food web (of interaction between different species in the agro-ecosystem, and of different seasons). This complex knowledge, of interacting, self-organising, self-maintaining, self-renewing and self-evolving systems, that farmers have contributed to over 10,000 years of the evolution of agriculture, is now being validated through agroecology, the truly scientific approach to food production.

Farmers have used available land and water to feed humanity for millennia, constantly evolving tastier, more nourishing varieties. Their success lies in their understanding of the earth, nature and her ecosystems, human beings, and all other species as autopoietic systems. A grandmother who knows how to transform the crops from our fields into a delicious nutritious meal, is a food scientist. An ayurvedic doctor is a scientist.

Indigenous people are scientists. Women are scientists. They have embodied, interactive and evolving knowledge.

We need to recognise the diversity of epistemologies and knowledge systems that have helped us in protecting the planet and ensuring our well-being. We need to unleash our diverse, interconnected intelligences to create another imagination, and through it another world, beyond the illusions and control of the 1%.

The ecology and economics of interconnectedness

Both ecology and economics are derived from the ancient Greek word 'oikos' which means 'home'. Ecology is the science of the household, while economics is supposed to be about the management of the household. When economics works against ecology, it results in the mismanagement of the earth, our home. The prevailing climate crisis, water crisis, biodiversity crisis, food crisis are the different symptoms of this mismanagement. We mismanage the earth and destroy her ecological processes when we do not recognise nature's capital as the real capital.

Food and agriculture are areas where we see clearly the failure of the industrial agriculture models imposed by global corporations. The so-called 'modern' food and agriculture system, based on chemicals and GMOs, may be presented as efficient and productive, but they use ten times more energy, have already destroyed 75 per cent of the planet's soil, water, and biodiversity, and are responsible for 50 per cent of the greenhouse gas emissions which are driving climate change.[10] While industrial agriculture is promoted as a solution to hunger, it is responsible for 75 per cent of all ecological and health problems prevealent at the global level. Hunger, malnutrition, obesity, diabetes, allergies, cancers, neurological disorders are intrinsic to the design of a greed-driven, toxin-based food system.[11]

Colonisation transforms abundance into scarcity, driven by the greed of a few. The story of the 1% is the story of greed without limits, without respect for the rights of others, without responsibility for the consequences of their actions. It is this contest between sharing and greed, between interconnectedness and privatisation, between Oneness and the 1% that lies at the crux of this volume.

In an economy dominated by the 1% consumerism rules, and the 99% are denied even the most basic sustainability rights, including the right to food, to water, and to work and livelihoods.

We are one earth family, we are interbeings

While pursuing my PhD, I became involved as a volunteer in the Chipko movement, a nonviolent, peaceful response to the large-scale deforestation that was taking place in the Garhwal Himalaya by peasant women from the region, who came out in defence of the forests. Chipko means 'to hug', 'to embrace'. Women declared that they would hug the trees to protect them—loggers would have to kill them before they felled the trees.

Logging had led to landslides and floods, and to the scarcity of water, fodder and fuel. Since women service these basic needs, scarcity meant longer walks for collecting water and firewood, and a heavier burden to bear. Women knew that the real value of forests was not the timber from a dead tree, but springs and streams, food for their cattle and fuel for their hearths. The folk songs of that period said,

These beautiful oaks and rhododendrons,
They give us cool water.
Don't cut these trees,
We have to keep them alive.

It took the 1978 Uttarkashi disaster, which created floods all the way to Calcutta in Bengal, for the Indian government to recognise that the women were right because the expenditure on flood relief far exceeded the revenues they were generating through timber. In 1981, in response to the Chipko movement, logging was banned above 1,000 kms in the Garhwal Himalaya. Today, government policy recognises that in the fragile Himalayas conservation maximises the ecological services of the forest.

The women activists of Chipko became my professors in biodiversity and ecology. I have always said that I received one PhD on the Foundations of Quantum Theory from the University of Western Ontario in Canada, and a second one on ecology from the forests of the Himalaya and women of the Chipko movement. Both taught me about interconnectedness and non-seperability. The women of Chipko taught me about the relationship between forests, soil and water and women's sustenance economies; quantum theory taught me the four principles that have guided my thinking and my life's work—everything is interconnected, everything is potential, everything is indeterminate, there is no excluded middle; we are interbeings. The quantum world is not made up of fixed particles, but of potential. A quanta can be a wave or a particle. It is indeterminate, therefore, uncertain. It is non-separable, non-local. Therefore, action at a distance becomes possible. And contrary to the mechanistic ideal of nature-human separation, the observer 'creates' the observed. An interactive, interrelated world becomes possible.

While the mechanical view forms the basis of mastery and conquest over nature, and hence is at the root of the ecological crisis, quantum and ecological paradigms have the same underlying understanding of an interconnected universe.

From the trees we learn unconditional love and unconditional giving. From the dry leaves that fall we learn about the cycle of life, the law of return, as leaves become humus and soil, protecting the earth, recycling nutrition and water, recharging springs, wells and streams. Forests also teach us 'enoughness', as the principle of equity, enjoying the gifts of nature without exploitation and accumulation.

The diversity, harmony and self-sustaining nature of the forest formed the organisational principles guiding Indian civilisation; the 'aranya samskriti' (roughly translatable as 'the culture of the forest') was not a condition of primitiveness, but one of conscious choice.

My own biological life and ecological journey started in the forests of the Himalaya. My father was a forest conservator, and my mother chose to be a farmer after becoming a refugee following the tragic partition of India in 1947. It is through the Himalayan forests and ecosystems that most of my learning of ecology took place.

The lessons I learnt about diversity in the Himalayan forests have been transferred to the protection of biodiversity on our farms. Navdanya, the movement for biodiversity conservation and organic farming that I started in 1987, has saved seeds through creating community seed banks, and has helped farmers make the transition from fossil fuel and chemical-based monocultures to biodiverse ecological systems nourished by the sun and the soil. Biodiversity has been my teacher of abundance and freedom, of cooperation and mutual giving.

But the Chipko movement of the 1970s was not India's first. In an earlier Chipko, in 1730, in Rajasthan, 363 people sacrificed their lives to protect their sacred khejri tree (*prosopis cineraria*). The khejri stands as a sentinel in the desert landscape of Rajasthan, as its poem. It is vital to sustainability in a desert ecosystem, as a source of fuel, firewood and organic fertiliser. Its fruit, saangri, is rich in protein and is used to prepare pickles and vegetables. The shade of the khejri conserves moisture in the soil, and offers protection from the scorching sun to humans and animals.

The khejri was declared a sacred tree by Jambhoji, a saint, who founded the Bishnoi faith. Bishnoi means 29, and the faith is based on 29 rules of compassion and conservation. During a discourse to one of his disciples, Jambhoji said,

> Do not fell a green tree,
> This is a charter for everyone.
> Be always ready to save (trees),
> This is the duty of everyone.

For over two centuries, people living in accordance with these tenets created flourishing groves of trees and protected wildlife in the Rajasthan desert. One such Bishnoi village was Khejarli, situated 20 kilometres south of Jodhpur. When the king's palace was being built, a court official, Girdhar Das, was made responsible for procuring firewood to burn the limestone required to make lime. A group arrived at the house of Amrita Devi, at home with her three young daughters, Asu Bai, Ratni Bai and Bhagni Bai. Amrita Devi had a giant khejri growing at her doorstep. When the king's men started to cut the tree, she tried to stop them, saying the cutting of green trees was against her religion. She said she would rather sacrifice her life than sacrifice the tree. She offered her head, and the axeman cut off her head. Her daughters followed; they too were beheaded. The news spread like wildfire, and Bishnois from 84 villages gathered in Khejrali to join the stream of volunteers to protect the trees; 363 people sacrificed their lives, and the sacred khejri trees were saved.

When the king of Jodhpur heard about this sacrifice, he immediately issued a royal decree making the cutting of green trees and the hunting of animals within the revenue boundaries of Bishnoi villages, a crime. To this day, the Bishnois take people to court for killing their sacred species—the khejri, the black buck, and the great Indian bustard. As Rajasthan is a fragile desert, ecological survival has been possible because of the conservation ethics built into everyday rules for the protection of life.

The forest thus nurtured an ecological civilisation in the most fundamental sense of harmony with nature. Such knowledge that came from participation in the life of the forest was not just the substance of the *Aranyakas*, or forest texts, but also of the everyday beliefs of tribal and peasant society. The ongoing struggle of the Dongria Kondh in Odisha to save their sacred mountain, Niyamgiri, from mining for bauxite is part of this ancient tradition.

Today, as the ecological crisis deepens with forest fires in the Arctic, floods in the desert of Ladakh, and in China and Pakistan, we can find renewed inspiration and a vision for the future from worldviews that see nature as alive and as the very basis of human life. We can thank Amrita Devi and the 363 Bishnois who sacrificed their lives so that the trees, the earth, and we, may live.

The empire of the 1%: separation, violence, colonisation, extractivism, extinction

Separation is an illusion, is violence

Oneness, as unity within the earth family and the human family, is very different from 'the status quo'—the rule of the 1% (or 0.01%, or 0.001%)—which uses the ideology of separation to extract, exterminate and push species, cultures and communities to extinction, while also dividing us as a society, and alienating us from our humanity. The rule of the 1% is based on separation—from the earth and from society.

It is an illusion, a construct, an assumption built by the powerful, the dominant, to colonise, conquer, exploit, divide, rule over other beings and other humans. Separation is violence.

Separation is a worldview, a paradigm, an ideology, a way of seeing and a way of shaping the world, both in our minds and in nature and society, through violence. It moulds our ideas of knowledge, of science and technology, of the economy, production and consumption, of democracy and freedom, and of who we are, our identities, our purpose, of why we are on the earth.

The three big separations that have brought us to the verge of extinction as a species are the separation of humans from nature; the separation of humans from each other through divisions of class, religion, race, and gender; and the separation of the Self from our integral, interconnected being.

The first separation, of humans from nature, creates eco-apartheid. It separates the soil and the earth from our bodies and our minds. It separates the interconnected aspects of nature, dividing it up into fragmented, separable parts to be exploited, owned, traded, destroyed, wasted. It separates the 1%

from society. It separates the powerful from the consequences of their actions, creating the possibility of zero liability, zero responsibility. Separation allows a handful of men to imagine they are masters of the universe, who can conquer, own, manipulate and control nature and society for accumulating power and wealth without limits.

Colonialism led to the violent separation of people from their land, resources and territories. It continues to this day, as greed for land and water, and for timber and minerals feeds an extractive economy, while globalisation's rules for deregulation and the 'ease of doing business' make uprooting communities easy.[12] Old colonialism violently appropriated the wealth and resources of societies in Africa, Asia, and the Americas, and transferred it to Europe. God and religion were invoked, through the narrative of the 'civilising mission', to transform these illegal acts and crimes against humanity into the rights of European kings and queens, and bandits, invaders and traders under their protection.

If the British grabbed land and institionalised lagaan (tax) in India, the contemporary 1% are using 'intellectual property' to create monopolies over our seeds and food, our communications, our financial transactions, and our friendships. The age of the robber barons began with the age of oil, which was also the age of the rule of money. Standard Oil, set up by the Rockefellers, shaped the economic, political, technological world of today.[13]

Today, the real owners of pirated wealth, derived from a predatory economic system, have constructed legal forms to protect themselves, and to escape liability. At the forefront of creating illusions for amassing wealth is the 'digital' world which is mining 'data', mining social relations (through Facebook), mining real economies, for profit. Digital money is replacing the real wealth of people; e-commerce is displacing real commerce. Goods are still produced and distributed, albeit at higher ecological and social costs. Meanwhile, local economies, local businesses, and local communities are slowly disappearing.

The money machine, facilitated by the mechanical mind, allows the 1% to extract wealth from nature and society, defining their 'extractivism' as scientific, economic and human 'progress'. The denial of self-organisation, intelligence, creativity, freedom, potential, autopoietic evolution and non-separability in nature and society is the basis of the domination, exploitation and colonisation, enslavement and extraction, of nature and diverse cultures, of women and indigenous people, of farmers and workers through brute power and violence. The result is an ecological crisis; a human crisis of hunger and poverty, of deepening inequality, of marginalisation and alienation, of uprooting, dispossession, and the creation of refugees. Linear, extractive systems based on violence are at the root of economic inequality, and the polarisation of society into the 1% and the 99%; they are the basis of new forms of enslavement, and an unprecedented exercise of disposability and extermination.

What we are witnessing is an intensification of the epistemic, ontological, ecological, political, economic, social and cultural violence of a dominant system based on the economic paradigm of the 1%. Economic polarisation is not just amplifying the deep inequality between the 1% and the 99%, it is brutalising the excluded, and uprooting millions from their homes.

Being uprooted is considerd to be the road to progress. That is why displacement is the most violent aspect of the current model of 'development'. Every dam, every highway, every expanding city is predicated on a violent land-grab which results in protracted conflict. Forced separation from our homes due to wars, often a consequence of the extraction of resources and of ecological degradation, is becoming the dominant condition of our times. Images of refugees from Mexico, Syria, Africa are a reflection of this brutal uprooting. According to the United Nations High Commissioner for Refugees (UNHCR), there are 65.6 million forcibly displaced people in the world today. And this number will grow as distorted economic 'development' and wars over resources intensify.

The second separation, of humans from each other, creates deliberate divisions within society, engineered along the lines of constructed inequality, based on gender, race, religion, and wealth, and the conscious implementation of a divide and rule policy to maintan economic power. Our rich diversities are being turned into the basis of our conflicts. An economy of greed is spinning off a politics of hate and fear, threatening democracy and our humanity.

As the 2016 US election showed, the 1% controls electoral democracy, extracts our intelligence and our autonomy to manipulate Big Data through artificial intelligence. Not only have the constructs that govern us and control our minds and our hearts separated us from nature, they have separated us from each other, and even from our being.

The third separation is from our sense of self, our false, engineered sense of being. For the powerful, it translates into uncontrollable greed and the search for unlimited, unregulated power. For the oppressed, it creates insecurity, fear, hate—for the other and oneself. Violence becomes all-pervasive and structural, replicated everyday in our ways of thinking, and in the economic and political systems.

The 1% essentially use separation to extract wealth and then use integration among and within themselves to restrict the concentration of the wealth. Different sectors of the economy are being merged for deeper and wider control and higher profits. Biotechnology, information technology (IT) and financial technology have merged and become one. Giant corporations are merging to create bigger cartels.

Separation, the mechanical mind, and mechanical intelligence

The world we have created is a product of our thinking. It cannot be changed without changing our thinking.

—Albert Einstein

The mechanical mind measures, predicts, and approaches knowing, but cannot actually *know* because knowledge, by its very nature, is pluralistic. Privileging one system over all others, and elevating reductionism as the only legitimate model of knowledge, leads to violence against science itself. This epistemic violence is now being combined with the violence of corporate interests to viciously attack all scientific traditions, including those that have evolved from within western science and have, through autopoietic epistemic evolution, transcended the limiting mechanistic worldview. Science as knowledge is being attacked so that Coroprate Science, based on 'alternative facts' and 'post truth', and spun by the PR machine of Big Money and corrupted governments, can be used as a colonising tool.

The creation of the mechanical mind is based on the construction of multiple separations. It separates soil from plants, by defining soil as an empty container for receiving chemical fertilisers, and plants as machines that run on fertiliser fuel. It separates food from health. It separates land from air, and land use from atmospheric pollution and climate change. It separates knowledge and intelligence from the processes of life and living, and reduces knowledge to information and data. It separates genes from the self-organised living organisms, and falsely assigns creative power to those who manipulate genes. It reduces life to 'intellectual property', to be owned and monopolised, even if species are pushed to extinction and farmers are driven to suicide.

According to the *Manifesto on the Future of Knowledge Systems* by the International Commission on the Future of Food and Agriculture,[14]

> Consciously or unconsciously, the world has been equated in our minds to a huge machine, free to be improved and modified by humans. Just as machines are assembled through the manipulation of their components, the same, we thought, can be done with the whole world, both living and non-living. This has led to the disruption of fragile ecological processes vital for human survival. It was assumed that complete knowledge of the whole could be attained simply by the knowledge of its individual parts. This method, reducing the whole to a composite of its parts, was elevated from a methodology with a practical scope, to a theory and even an ideology, and the metaphor 'natural systems are *like* machines' progressively became the much more radical 'natural systems *are* machines'.

Ernesto Guevera, a peasant leader from Mexico, has called a mechanical ideology 'epistemic racism'; one could also call it 'epistemic sexism'.

The urge to impose uniformity in agriculture as well as artificial, fixed, narrow, negative 'identities', in contest and conflict with each other, is an impulse of the mechanical mind. It assumes that there are 'experts' with 'objective' knowledge, who are separate from, and superior to, ordinary men, women, peasants, workers, and experts of other knowledge traditions, such as ayurveda and agroecology, for instance. This separation is a 'knowledge apartheid'.

The mechanical mind is also a militarised mind. It is based on violence and leads to violence. It is ontologically violent because it declares nature as dead; it is epistemically violent because it destroys our capacity to think and act as part of nature, to be co-creators and nonviolent; it is ecologically violent, because through its ignorance, it disrupts processes that maintain the life of organisms, ecosystems, and the earth herself; it is socially violent because it is blind to, and outlaws, the embodied knowledge of women, peasants and indigenous cultures that the world so desperately needs today to heal the planet and society.

The mechanical mind is a privatising mind, it contributes to enclosures of nature's commons, social commons, and the knowledge commons, promoting biopiracy. While appropriating, pirating and patenting traditional knowledge, it simultaneously constructs an artificial wall or 'creation boundary'. Traditional knowledge is presented as 'innovation' and 'invention', and privatised via patenting.

The mechanical mind locks causality into the straitjacket of linear, mechanical cause and effect, and action limited to contact. However, in living systems, causality is systemic, and properties and behaviours depend on context, on relationship, on complexity. It is four dimensional causality, the integrated, non-separability of living processes in space and time. Linear causality, on the one hand, allows claims to be made linking specific tools to complex, multi-causal phenomena. In the Green Revolution narrative, Norman Borlaug's 'miracle' dwarf wheats, bred with chemicals, increased food production in India; but as our studies show, an increase in the output of rice and wheat can be accounted for by increasing the area under production, and improving irrigation. So *land* and *water* contributed to higher production, but this was falsely associated with *new seeds* and *chemicals*. Linear causality when applied to complex systems allows corporations producing harmful chemicals and GMOs to deny the harmful impacts of their products. By falsely reducing complex interactive living processes to 'one cause, one effect' the mechanical mind creates a false causality. This is how 'safety' issues are manipulated and hazards are denied. This is also how systems' effectiveness in paradigms based on systems science are ignored and denied.

The mechanical mind conveniently externalises costs to society and nature through its linear constructed narrative of conquest, mastery, progress. It separates 'cause' as a system of structural violence from the effect of violence and harm to nature and people. In the process, it creates a system where the powerful, who shape and use mechanistic tools for control, appropriate absolute rights with absolute irresponsibility.

Ontological schizophrenia is another characteristic of the mechanical mind. The knowledge of how to make a product or develop a technology is separated from awareness of the impact of that product or technology on nature and society. This translates into a separation of rights from responsibilities. GMOs represent ontological schizophrenia in the extreme. When it comes to claiming intellectual property rights to seeds and lifeforms, the GMO is claimed to be novel, an invention; when it comes to taking responsibility for biosafety, the impact of the GMO on the environment and health becomes 'substantially equivalent' to naturally occurring organisms and existing seeds and organisms. The same entity is simultaneously constructed as novel and as a totally new invention when it comes to rights, ownership, and collection of royalties, and as natural when it comes to avoiding responsibility for harm caused to nature and people. Furthermore, the rush to commodify and commercialise a product or technology is the manufacture of systemic ignorance. Ignorance is the absence of knowledge, it is not science. True science requires a knowledge of systems.

We are witnessing not just the merger of the giant corporations, which have their roots in the Toxic Cartel of the World Wars, but a convergence of sectors in one unbroken continuum and consolidation of destructive and violent power—from biotechnology in agriculture, to information technology and financial technologies. The coercion used against the diversity of indigenous cultures and their knowledge throughout colonial history is now being directed at citizens worldwide. The intelligence of nature and people is being replaced by 'intelligence' as surveillance—whether surveillance by Monsanto over farmers to prevent them from saving seeds, or surveillance by Facebook and Google over our everyday lives, or the surveillance of the corporate state over citizens seeking freedom.

The latest endeavour of the mechanical mind is to reduce the world to fragments of information, broken down further into data. Data are being treated as the new raw material and simultaneously being given the status of 'intelligence'. However, data is not knowledge, and data processing is not intelligence.

Breaking free of the mechanical mind has now become an ecological and political imperative. The duty to care, the courage to stop the harm being caused by the 1% to the earth and its beings, is part of life and living.

The Hopi describe the phenomenon of destroying everything

that sustains a society as *powaqqatsi*. If corporations have their way our fragile web of life will be poisoned, the diversity of species will be driven to extinction, people will lose all freedoms—to their seeds, to their food, their knowledge and decision-making—and all social relations will be ruptured.

The deep crises of exclusion and extinction invite us to unleash the living intelligence of all beings to heal and rejuvenate the planet and ourselves. This volume explores these processes and the economic model that is being imposed on the world, creating a 1% economy that has resulted in inhuman inequalities and a rapid and deep enclosure of the democratic space. Through what is happening to our planet, our resources, our money, our biodiversity, our food, we expose how these systems, controlled by Big Money work, and describe the future they are trying to engineer, based on their vision of One Science, One Agriculture, One History, One per cent. It also addresses the urgent need for creating alternatives to the Big Money world so that the rights of the earth, and of humanity, can be defended, reclaimed, deepened and enlarged, and we can foresee a future based on freedom and democracy.

The awareness of our real identity, as earth citizens and members of the earth family, is the beginning of the Resurgence of Real Intelligence, Real Seed, Real Food, Real Wealth, Real Freedom. It is the path of liberation from the rule of the 1% that cripples our imagination and enslaves us.

Endnotes

[1] 'What is Happening to Agrobiodiversity?' http://www.fao.org/docrep/007/y5609e/y5609e02.htm.
[2] *Universal Declaration of Rights of Mother Earth*, http://therightsofnature.org/universal-declaration/; Valerie Cabanes, *Rights for Planet Earth: End to*

Crimes Against Nature, http://valeriecabanes.eu/rights-for-planet-earth-book-release-in-india/.

[3] The original definition can be found in Humberto Maturana and Francisco Varela, *Autopoiesis and Cognition: The Realization of the Living*. First edition published in 1973. Second edition, Robert Cohen and Marx Wartofsky (Eds.) *Boston Studies in the Philosophy of Science*. Dordrecht: D. Reidel Publishing Co., 1980.

[4] Bruno Latour, 'On Interobjectivity', *Mind, Culture, and Activity*. 3, 4 (1996), pp. 228-45. http.//www.bruno-latour.fr/sites/default/files/63-INTEROBJECTS-GB.pdf.

[5] J.C. Bose. See, among others, *Plant response as a means of Physiological investigation*. London: Longmans, Green and Co., 1906; *Life Movements in Plants (Vol. I)*, first published in 1918 and reprinted in 1985; *Life Movements in Plants (Vol. II)*, published in 1919; *Nervous Mechanisms of Plants*, published in 1926; and *Growth and Tropic Movements of Plants*. London: Longmans, Green and Co., 1929.

[6] J.A. Shapiro, 'Bacteria are Small But Not Stupid: Cognition, Natural Genetic Engineering and Socio-Bacteriology', *Studies in History and Philosophy of Biological and Biomedical Sciences*. 38, 4 (2007), pp. 807-19; Epub, November 19, 2007.

[7] André Leu, *Poisoning Our Children*. Greeley: Acres, 2018; and Stafanie Seneff in Vandana Shiva (Ed.) *Seed Sovereignty and Food Security: Women in the Vanguard*. New Delhi: Women Unlimited, 2015.

[8] Yaneer Bar-Yam, *Dynamics of Complex Systems*. Massachusetts: Addison Wesley, 1997. http://fernandonogueiracosta.files.wordpress.com/2015/08/yaneer-bar-yam-dynamics-of-complex-systems.pdf.

[9] Carl R. Woese, 'A New Biology for a New Century', *Microbiology And Molecular Biology Reviews*. 68, 2 (2004), pp. 173–186. http://mmbr.asm.org/content/68/2/173.full.

[10] Vandana Shiva, *Who Really Feeds the World?* New Delhi: Women Unlimited, 2017.

[11] *ANNAM: Food as Health*. New Delhi: Navdanya, 2017. See also, Daniel Moss and Mark Bittman, 'Bringing Farming Back to Nature', *The New York Times*. http://www.nytimes.com/2018/06/26/opinion/farming-organic-nature-movement.html. Published on June 26, 2018.

[12] Charles Beebe, '2016 Deadliest Yet for Environmental Defenders', *pantheism.com*. https://pantheism.com/2016-deadliest-yet-environmental-defenders/. Published on July 13, 2017.

[13] Leonardo Maugeri, *The Age of Oil: The Mythology, History, and Future of the World's Most Controversial Resource*. Connecticut: Globe Pequot, 2007; Dale Allen Pfeiffer, *The End of the Oil Age*. Napa: Lulu Press, 2004.

[14] *Manifesto On The Future Of Knowledge Systems: Knowledge Sovereignty For A Healthy Planet*, International Commission on the Future of Food and Agriculture, 2009, http://www.swaraj.org/manifesto_future.pdf.

2 The Money Machine of the 1%

1% is not just a number, it is a system, an economic system shaped by the rich and powerful, where unbridled greed and accumulation are seen as virtues to be rewarded by society, instead of aberrations which must be kept within limits through social and democratic processes. It is a model in which who produces, what is produced, or whether anything at all is in fact produced, are questions that disappear from the economic equation. They are replaced by tools of money-making, money making money, or what Aristotle called 'chrematistics'. It effects an economic apartheid between the haves and havenots, which translates into an ecological apartheid between the lives and live-nots, not just in the human family, but in the earth family. The rise of the 1% embodies a will to exclude, an urge to exterminate. Its inevitable consequences are ecocide and genocide.

The Oxfam report, 'An Economy for the 1%', reveals that the richest 1% own as much as 3.6 billion people do—the bottom 50% of humanity.[1] While the wealth of the richest 62 people in the world increased by more than 45 per cent between 2010 and 2015—an increase of more than half a trillion dollars, from $542 billion to $1.76 trillion—the wealth of the bottom half fell by just over a trillion dollars over the same period—a drop of 38 per cent. In 2010, 388 individuals had as much wealth as the poorest half; in 2011, the figure was 177; in 2012, it dropped to 159; in 2013, it went down further to 92; in 2014, it was 80; and in 2017, the figure came down to just eight.[2]

Today, the financial sector, where the rich make money out of money, has increased to 15 per cent of the GDP in most countries worldwide, including India and the US. As the Oxfam report indicates, in the economy of the 1%, 437 of the largest corporations in 2014 were financial, and their assets were five

The Money Machine of the 1%

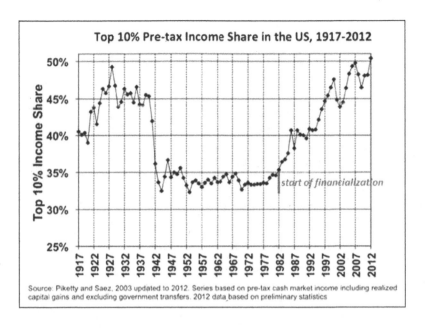

Top 10% Pre-tax Income Share in the US, 1917-2012

Source: Piketty and Saez, 2003 updated to 2012. Series based on pre-tax cash market income including realized capital gains and excluding government transfers. 2012 data based on preliminary statistics

times greater than those of corporations in other sectors. Following the 2008 financial crisis, the richest 1% captured 95% of the world's growth, reports *The Wall Street Journal*. While ordinary people lost jobs, homes, pensions and security, those gambling in the financial markets got richer.

Financial deregulation, which included removing the separation between savings and investment, created an economy based on speculation, with the financial economy overtaking the real economy and depleting it of oxygen in multiple ways.

From 2009, when the Great Recession officially ended, through 2012, the top 1 per cent of Americans raked in 95 cents out of every dollar of increased income. Almost one-third of the national increase went to just 16,000 households, the top 1 per cent of the top 1 per cent, as Thomas Piketty and Emmanuel Saez's analysis of Internal Revenue Service (IRS) data shows.[3]

The Top 100 Moneymakers[4]

Rank	Name	Net Worth	Age	Source	Country of Citizenship	Commodity
#1	Bill Gates	$75 B	60	Microsoft	United States	
#2	Amancio Ortega	$67 B	80	Zara	Spain	Cotton
#3	Warren Buffett	$60.8 B	85	Berkshire Hathaway	United States	Cotton
#4	Carlos SlimHelú	$50 B	76	telecom	Mexico	Food
#5	Jeff Bezos	$45.2 B	52	Amazon.com	United States	
#6	Mark Zuckerberg	$44.6 B	31	Facebook	United States	
#7	Larry Ellison	$43.6 B	71	Oracle	United States	
#8	Michael Bloomberg	$40 B	74	Bloomberg LP	United States	
#9	Charles Koch	$39.6 B	80	diversified	United States	Oil
#9	David Koch	$39.6 B	75	diversified	United States	Oil
#11	Liliane Bettencourt	$36.1 B	93	L'Oreal	France	
#12	Larry Page	$35.2 B	43	Google	United States	
#13	Sergey Brin	$34.4 B	42	Google	United States	
#14	Bernard Arnault	$34 B	67	LVMH	France	
#15	Jim Walton	$33.6 B	67	Wal-Mart	United States	Food
#16	Alice Walton	$32.3 B	66	Wal-Mart	United States	Food

The Money Machine of the 1%

Rank	Name	Net Worth	Age	Source	Country of Citizenship	Commodity
#17	S. Robson Walton	$31.9 B	71	Wal-Mart	United States	Food
#18	Wang Jianlin	$28.7 B	61	real estate	China	
#19	Jorge Paulo Lemann	$27.8 B	76	beer	Brazil	Food
#20	Li Ka-shing	$27.1 B	87	diversified	Hong Kong	
#21	Beate Heister & Karl Albrecht Jr.	$25.9 B	—	supermarkets	Germany	Food
#22	Sheldon Adelson	$25.2 B	82	casinos	United States	
#23	George Soros	$24.9 B	85	hedge funds	United States	
#24	Phil Knight	$24.4 B	78	Nike	United States	
#25	David Thomson	$23.8 B	58	media	Canada	
#26	Steve Ballmer	$23.5 B	60	Microsoft	United States	
#27	Forrest Mars, Jr.	$23.4 B	84	candy	United States	Food
#27	Jacqueline Mars	$23.4 B	76	candy	United States	Food
#27	John Mars	$23.4 B	79	candy	United States	Food
#30	Maria Franca Fissolo	$22.1 B	98	Nutella, chocolates	Italy	Food
#31	Lee Shau Kee	$21.5 B	88	real estate	Hong Kong	
#32	Stefan Persson	$20.8 B	68	H&M	Sweden	Cotton
#33	Jack Ma	$20.5 B	51	Alibaba	China	
#34	Theo Albrecht, Jr.	$20.3 B	65	Aldi, Trader Joe's	Germany	Food

Rank	Name	Net Worth	Age	Source	Country of Citizenship	Commodity
#35	Michael Dell	$19.8 B	51	Dell	United States	
#36	Mukesh Ambani	$19.3 B	58	petrochemicals, oil & gas	India	Oil
#37	Leonardo Del Vecchio	$18.7 B	80	eyeglasses	Italy	
#38	Susanne Klatten	$18.5 B	53	BMW, pharma ceuticals	Germany	Auto
#39	Georg Schaeffler	$18.1 B	51	ball bearings	Germany	Auto
#40	Paul Allen	$17.5 B	63	Microsoft, investments	United States	
#41	Prince Alwaleed Bin Talal Alsaud	$17.3 B	61	investments	Saudi Arabia	
#42	Joseph Safra	$17.2 B	77	banking	Brazil	
#43	Carl Icahn	$17 B	80	investments	United States	
#44	Laurene Powell Jobs	$16.7 B	52	Apple, Disney	United States	
#45	Dilip Shanghvi	$16.7 B	60	pharmaceuticals	India	Pharma
#46	Ma Huateng	$16.6 B	44	internet media	China	
#47	Dieter Schwarz	$16.4 B	76	retail	Germany	Food
#48	Ray Dalio	$15.6 B	66	hedge funds	United States	
#49	Stefan Quandt	$15.6 B	49	BMW	Germany	Auto
#50	James Simons	$15.5 B	77	hedge funds	United States	
#51	Aliko Dangote	$15.4 B	59	cement, sugar, flour	Nigeria	Food
#52	Michael Otto	$15.4 B	73	retail, real estate	Germany	Food

The Money Machine of the 1%

Rank	Name	Net Worth	Age	Source	Country of Citizenship	Commodity
#53	Len Blavatnik	$15.3 B	58	diversified	United States	
#54	Donald Bren	$15.1 B	83	real estate	United States	
#55	Azim Premji	$15 B	70	software services	India	
#56	Serge Dassault	$14.7 B	91	aviation	France	
#57	Tadashi Yanai	$14.6 B	67	retail	Japan	Cotton
#58	Cheng Yu-tung	$14.5 B	90	diversified	Hong Kong	Banking
#58	Hinduja family	$14.5 B	–	Hinduja Group	United Kingdom	Banking
#60	Leonid Mikhelson	$14.4 B	60	gas, chemicals	Russia	Oil
#60	David & Simon Reuben	$14.4 B	73	investments, real estate	United Kingdom	Property
#62	Stefano Pessina	$13.4 B	74	drugstores	Italy	Pharma
#63	Mikhail Fridman	$13.3 B	51	oil, banking, telecom	Russia	
#64	Dietrich Mateschitz	$13.2 B	71	Red Bull	Austria	
#65	Abigail Johnson	$13.1 B	54	money management	United States	Banking
#66	Kjeld Kirk Kristiansen	$13.1 B	68	Lego	Denmark	
#67	Joseph Lau	$13.1 B	64	real estate	Hong Kong	Property
#68	Gerald Cavendish Grosvenor	$13 B	64	real estate	United Kingdom	Property
#68	Thomas & Raymond Kwok	$13 B	–	real estate	Hong Kong	Property
#68	Marcel Herrmann Telles	$13 B	66	beer	Brazil	Food

Rank	Name	Net Worth	Age	Source	Country of Citizenship	Commodity
#71	Henry Sy	$12.9 B	91	SM Investments Corporation	Philippines	Banking
#72	Steve Cohen	$12.7 B	60	hedge funds	United States	Banking
#73	Pallonji Mistry	$12.5 B	86	construction	Ireland	Property
#73	Hans Rausing	$12.5 B	90	packaging	Sweden	Food
#73	Alisher Usmanov	$12.5 B	62	steel, telecom, investments	Russia	
#76	Charlene de Carvalho-Heineken	$12.3 B	61	Heineken	Netherlands	Food
#77	Charles Ergen	$12.2 B	63	satellite TV	United States	Media
#78	Ronald Perelman	$12.1 B	73	leveraged buyouts	United States	Banking
#78	Vladimir Potanin	$12.1 B	55	metals	Russia	
#80	Stephen Ross	$12 B	75	real estate	United States	Property
#81	Patrick Soon-Shiong	$11.9 B	64	pharmaceuticals	United States	Pharma
#82	Masayoshi Son	$11.7 B	58	internet, telecom	Japan	
#82	Heinz Hermann Thiele	$11.7 B	75	brakes	Germany	Auto
#84	Francois Pinault	$11.5 B	79	retail	France	Cotton
#85	David Tepper	$11.4 B	58	hedge funds	United States	Banking
#85	Gennady Timchenko	$11.4 B	63	oil & gas	Russia	Oil
#87	Carlos Alberto Sicupira	$11.3 B	68	beer	Brazil	Food
#88	Shiv Nadar	$11.1 B	70	software services	India	

The Money Machine of the 1%

Rank	Name	Net Worth	Age	Source	Country of Citizenship	Commodity
#89	Thomas Peterffy	$11.1 B	71	discount brokerage	United States	
#90	Robin Li	$11 B	47	internet search	China	
#90	Alain Wertheimer	$11 B	67	Chanel	France	Cotton
#90	Gerard Wertheimer	$11 B	65	Chanel	France	Cotton
#93	Alexey Mordashov	$10.9 B	50	steel, investments	Russia	Mining
#94	Elon Musk	$10.7 B	44	Tesla Motors	United States	Auto
#94	Charoen Sirivadhanabhakdi	$10.7 B	71	beverages	Thailand	Food
#96	Petr Kellner	$10.6 B	51	banking, insurance	Czech Republic	
#96	Rupert Murdoch	$10.6 B	85	media	United States	
#98	Viktor Vekselberg	$10.5 B	59	metals, energy	Russia	Mining
#99	Lukas Walton	$10.4 B	29	Wal-Mart	United States	Food
#100	Eric Schmidt	$10.2 B	60	Google	United States	Food

The income changes for the vast majority are just as revealing. The bottom 90 per cent saw their average incomes rise 8.8 per cent in 1934 over the previous year (the year 1933 marked the beginning of recovery from the Great Depression), and in 2012, the same statistical group had to get by on 15.7 per cent less than in 2009. Piketty points out that the 1% made more money from capital investments, whereas others get money from wages; because capital income is unequally distributed, it leads to growing inequality. He shows that whether capital is taxed or not, inequality will grow under current policies because savings from current wages and salaries cannot grow as much as returns on existing wealth. According to Piketty, the process of accumulating 'becomes more rapid and inegalitarian as the return on capital rises and the [overall economic] growth rate falls.'

The 1% economy is not just a system of economic inequality; it has implications for the planet, for society, and for democracy, because it symbolises a system of thought and an intellectual paradigm, based on a worldview of separation, extraction and extermination.

The Robber Barons of today are in information technology and in finance, agriculture and biotechnology. And the three are converging in the digital economy, through digital tools. Nature is made an enemy, and humans start to race against nature. Those in the global casino see nature and life as a 'tyranny'.

In their book, *The Fisherman and the Rhinoceros: How International Finance Shapes Everyday Life*,[5] Eric Briys and Francois de Varenne describe what they call 'the tyranny of the real economy'. What the financial economy enables us to do, they argue, is to break free of that tyranny. Risks can be moved through the use of derivatives not only to the right people, but also moved forward into the future to wait for the right time! By trading swaps for swaps, bundling debts and re-selling them as assets, and by selling derivatives on these assets, risks can be moved around until they are in exactly the right place, as determined by the market. Among examples of businesses that have successfully broken free of this tyranny, the authors mention two: Enron and mortgage-backed securities.

But Enron collapsed, and the subprime crisis triggered by the securitisation of mortgages left the world with the 2008 financial crisis. As Justin Podur writes in *Counter Punch*, 'The question for a society is whether we want our lives to be devoted to saving elites from the monstrous power gambles for obscene amounts of money, or whether we would rather absorb the more moderate risks that everyday people have to take seeking decent survival. That would not automatically happen even if the rules were changed to reassert the "tyranny of the real economy", but would require a very different sort of real economy.'[6]

Corporations and sectors that did not exist a few decades ago, account for the fastest growth in profits today, and for the largest number of the New Moghuls. First, the billionaires and robber barons who emerged over the last two decades are creating their own investment strategies and rental economies, with rents collected through royalties on patents: on seeds; on software; on algorithms to process Big Data. Speculation, predation and rents are their primary sources of profits. Second, with this unreasonable concentration of wealth in the hands of the1%—which is 'wealth without work' and multiplies at much faster rates than that at which the real economy, based on real production, can grow—the investment funds owned by the 1% can buy up large shares in big corporations and drive mergers in order to further multiply profits. This is how the merger between Monsanto and Bayer is taking place. Finally, the 1%

is also creating mergers between those technology spheres that were earlier separate. Thus, whereas information technology (IT) was separate from finance, was separate from biotechnology in agriculture, those boundaries are now gone. IT, through digitisation, now drives both the financial world and the economy, and it is driving the next phase of industrial agriculture, described as Digital Agriculture and 'farming without farmers'.[7]

Money, a mere means of exchange of real goods and services, produced through real work, becomes 'capital', a mysterious force of creating wealth. 'Capital' then mutates into 'investment', which mutates, through multiple constructions into 'returns on investment', where those who do no real work but control wealth created through the exploitation of nature and of people, accumulate more wealth, and use that wealth to further exploit nature and society. The ecological crises grow. Poverty, misery, and exclusion grow.

Many intellectuals wonder how we got into this mess. A fashionable answer is 'neoliberalism'. But neoliberalism is nothing more than the economic paradigm naturalising the violent imposition of corporate rule and the rule of the 1%. It is true that contemporary corporate globalisation, based on the neoliberal paradigm, has created the huge power of a handful of corporations. But corporations have not always existed. They were created as an instrument of colonisation. They do not come into existence 'out of thin air', they are born out of contexts created by just the right amount of power and money, in the absence of democracy.

Neither neoliberalism, nor corporate globalisation are new. They began five centuries ago with the age of Columbus who had set out for India, but reached the Americas. His journey to plunder became the 'Discovery of America'. With the creation of the East India Company in 1600, specifically created to plunder India, the foundations of contemporary corporate rule and corporate globalisation were laid. The poverty created by corporate colonialism was then essentialised and separated from its causes, and, over the centuries, the disease has been offered as the cure. A myth has grown that only corporations can run an economy and only they can write the rules of the economy, of trade and commerce.

Aspects of life that were never part of commerce have been privatised under the new rules of 'free trade'. Seed became Monsanto's intellectual property, for which it collects royalties and rent. Food is now a commodity, traded by merchants of grain like Cargill, and transformed into junk by Coca-Cola and Pepsi, Nestlé and Kellog's.

Large corporations define freedom as 'free trade', which is corporate globalisation. The freedom of corporations and their masked owners is misused to destroy the earth's ecological fabric and the fabric of people's economies and societies. 'Free trade' rules are written by corporations to enlarge their freedom to commodify and privatise the last inch of land, the last drop of water, the last seed, the last serving of food, the last byte of information, the last bit of data, knowledge and imagination.

The deregulation of corporations, and the policing and criminalising of citizens, has enormous impact on our lives, livelihoods and freedoms. The consolidation and spread of corporate power, undermining the real economies that nourish and sustain people, is one impact. Another major consequence has been mutations in politics, with representative democracy moving rapidly from being 'of the people, by the people, for the people' to 'of the corporations, by the corporations, for the corporations'. Worse, the concentration of economic power in the hands of a small group of unelected, unaccountable individuals, translates into political power to influence governments, laws, and policies, to shape the future of our food and health and of the planet.

In India, the highest policy-making body, Niti Aayog (also serving executive functions), constitutes people whose only expertise is corporate 'free trade' and trade liberalisation. The promotion of imports when we don't need them; the undemocratic undermining of government institutions working as per the Constitution to protect the farmer's rights to seed, and people's rights to affordable and safe medicine; and pushing GMOs and hazardous medicines, are examples of corporate metrics outweighing real life. Niti Aayog has become a one-stop-shop for global corporate lobby groups to transform India's economy into their private (backyard) market. This is systemic corruption of our democracy and a recipe for destruction of people's economies.

The concentration of economic power and the systematic wipe-out of local economies creates unemployment, displacement and economic insecurity; these insecurities are then used by the powerful to divide societies along racial, ethnic and religious lines. The fragmentation and disintegration of societies is intimately linked to the extractive economic model of wealth accumulation by a few.

How the billionaires make money out of money, while controlling our real worlds and our lives

In 1994, Joel Kurtzman wrote,

> The financial economy is somewhere between 20 to 50 times larger than the real economy. It is not the economy of trade but of

speculation. Its commerce is in financial instruments. And while its ultra hi-tech infrastructure straddles the globe and moves several trillion dollars a day between the major and minor nodes of the network, it is largely unregulated. Few people realize money in its traditional sense has met its demise. Fewer still have paused to reflect on its imact.[8]

Corporate globalisation, and the World Bank and International Monetary Fund (IMF) driven structural adjustment programmes of the 1980s, led to the deregulation of financial markets in a number of countries. In retail banking, investment banks and stock brokers merged to create 'universal banks' which were free to deal in all forms of financial services, make investments in client companies, and function as much as possible as a 'one-stop' supplier of both retail and wholesale financial services; insurance; pension; mutual money market and hedge funds; loans; and credits and securities. By end-2001, the world's 15 largest financial services providers included four non-banks. In 1999, US President Bill Clinton signed into law the Gramm-Leach-Bliley Act (GLBA), which repealed some of the provisions of the Glass-Steagall Act.[9] Globalisation led to a significant internationalisation of financial markets, integrating the world into one financial system. By the 2000s, non-bank financial players had started to dominate the financial sector.[10]

Central banks determine (among other things) interest rates, nudging the economy along at the direction of their billionaire control agents. A little research into central banks indicates that they are primarily private enterprises, unaccountable to the people whose financial status they govern. It is clear that over the last three decades, central banks have pushed the agenda of the 1%; what needs to be examined carefully is the objective of the 1% in openly hijacking central banks.

What J.P. Morgan and John D. Rockefeller were to the Age of Robber Barons, Microsoft's Bill Gates and Berkshire Hathaway's Warren Buffett, as well as digital moguls like Mark Zuckerberg and Jeff Bezos are to the contemporary age of the rule of the 1%. Then as now, the super-rich used governments to write laws and rules to allow them to accumulate unlimited wealth; then as now, creating monopolies by enclosing the commons and killing competition is the strategy for becoming the 1%.

Gambling in the global casino while appropriating the wealth of people: the story of Buffett

The One Economy being built by Bill Gates and Warren Buffett and Big Money, is evidenced by the fact that the largest investment made by the Gates Foundation Trust, worth $11.8 billion in 2014, is in the US conglomerate, Berkshire Hathaway, whose Chief Executive Officer Warren Buffett—a trustee of the Gates Foundation—has donated billions to the Foundation Trust. (The BMGF Trust manages 'the investment assets and transfer[s] proceeds to the Foundation as necessary to achieve the foundation's charitable goals'. The Trust's biggest investment stakes are in Berkshire Hathaway.) Bill Gates also serves as a board member of Berkshire Hathaway which has 60 subsidiaries, mainly US-based, in sectors including agriculture, energy, retail, media, transportation, electronics, chemicals, jewellery, furniture and insurance. In our world this would qualify as conflict of interest, but in the world of Big Money it is 'innovation'.

How did Buffett get so 'rich'? Warren Buffett did not become rich with Berkshire Hathaway; he accumulated wealth through the Government Employees Insurance Company (GEICO).

44

He sold insurance to government employees, people who do not get to choose their insurance terms and conditions, its their employer who picks from among the choices that Buffett decides to offer. At a price of his choosing. Signed off by the regulator and paid for by the employee. A part of every government salary, automatically diverted as deductable insurance payment into Buffett's bank—an efficient, self-sustaining model of cash flow to Buffett-Land.

Casinos and insurance companies, the most lucrative enterprises in the world, use probability to earn profits. Legal language is employed to define events that rarely occur, and it is these improbable events that insurance contracts cover. Probability is used to earn profits by insuring events that rarely happen. And in case of a rare payout, Buffett loses the insured value, but retains a deductible which covers his costs allowing him to break-even. Break-odd is what happens when policies expire without a claim. According to the Chicago Mercantile Exchange data, collected over three years—1997 to 1999—76.5 per cent of all options, like insurance, expire worthless.[11] Additionally, 76.5 per cent of all government employees' insurance premiums go directly to the insurance company. Moreover, the cost of the payout due, if the insured event does occur, is pre-factored into the insurance premiums paid; the insurance company gets an insured income with 100 per cent certainty.

Selling options is what the Wall Street elite traders do. Billions are made on this every day. Warren Buffett's favourite 'option strategy', apparently, is 'selling puts'. Puts are options to 'buy into the outcome' (essentially, a contract). Let's be clear, it is not a bet on the outcome, which might involve some probability—it is merely a reservation at a table, at which the owner of the 'option' may choose to sit in the future.

In 1993, Buffett sold 50,000 put contracts, receiving $7.5 million in up front cash premiums. Simultaneously, he insured (possibly through his own insurance company) five million shares of Coca-Cola at $35 a share, shares he did not possess at the time. The value of each share then was $39, $4 above the insured value. If on the expiration date of the 50,000 put contracts, the value of Coca-Cola shares was higher than $35, Buffett would take home the $7.5 million premium and the insured friends of Buffett would have an option to purchase the shares at market value. If, however, Coca-Cola shares suddenly dropped in value he would get to keep the cash premium of $7.5 million, and still own five million shares, each purchased at $4 below market value. [12]

While global economies crashed and Greece and Portugal were imprisoned by loan terms, Warren Buffett was busy acquiring the Burlington Northern Santa Fe rail system on November 3, 2009. He sold 5.5 million put options to establish a stake in the company before he purchased the entire company and made it private. Then he withdrew his account and cashed in. He also sold put options on various stock indices around the world, raising $4.9 billion from the sale. [13]

Put option sellers are the sole survivors of an economic meltdown, their capital and interests insulated from the economy by the government. Just as during the meltdown of 2008.

Vanguard and the new armada of investment funds: how the 1% control the economy and giant corporations

'Fuck the EU.'

—Victoria Nuland, Assistant Secretary of State for European and Eurasian Affairs, United States Department of State

The Money Machine of the 1%

The above was said during a telephone conversation that took place between Nuland and the US Ambassador to Ukraine, on January 28, 2014. Victoria Nuland also has ties to the Vanguard Group, a major private financial institution; her assistant is an employee of Vanguard. Nuland orchestrated a regime change in Ukraine on February, 22, 2014, spending $5 billion to destabilise the country. Her assistant was arrested in Germany with 'billions' in counterfeit currency printed by the Vanguard Group in 2016.[14]

In an article, titled 'Vanguard Reaches $3 Trillion In Assets, Matching Entire Hedge-Fund Industry', by Kirsten Grind, *The Wall Street Journal* described the Vanguard Group as 'an asset manager selling index funds from a leafy suburb of Philadelphia [that] now has about the same amount of assets under management as the entire hedge fund industry'. With all that capital, Vanguard has grown into the owner of industry, within the economy at least. Moreover, its involvement with Academi and Greystone makes it a political institution as well. Academi (formerly Blackwater), which owns Greystone, is an American private military company founded in 1997 by former Navy SEAL officer Erik Prince.[15] Other large and unregulated institutions include Fidelity, BlackRock and State Street.

When we began writing this book in 2016 Vanguard was worth $3 trillion; by the time we started editing it in 2017, the Group's wealth had increased to $4.3 trillion. At the time of going to print in 2018 its assets jumped to $5.1 trillion.[16]

Vanguard is owned by its investors; it's a mask for the billionaires of the world. It was created in 1958 when Wellington Fund, established with $10,000 on December 27, 1928, by Walter Morgan, merged with Windsor Fund.[17] Today, Vanguard is a 118-funds family. In 1974, the Vanguard Group was formed, and its investors became its charter members, i.e., the owners.

As John Bogle, Chairman of Wellington Fund said,

While I was 'out' as Wellington Management's Chief Executive, I remained 'in' as Chairman and President of Wellington Fund and its sister funds. After eight months of laborious study and give-and-take, I was able to persuade the Fund Directors to retain me in my posts and build a small staff to administer the funds accounting, shareholder record keeping, and legal affairs. We formed a new corporation to handle these responsibilities, wholly owned by the funds themselves and operating on an at-cost basis—a truly mutual structure, unique in the industry. The name I chose for the new firm, of course, was Vangard—the Vanguard Group Inc.

The Group was named after Horatio Nelson' flagship vessel at the Battle of the Nile, the *HMS Vanguard*.

In 2003, Vanguard Wellington had assets amounting to $29,985; today, the Vanguard Group controls assets worth more than $5.1 trillion. This is the magic of financialisation. Between 1978 and 2003, the annual rate of return to investors was 13 per cent and the cumulative return was 2058 per cent. This was 2.6 per cent more annually, and 950 per cent more cumulatively, than rival funds.

Vanguard's website states:

Unlike any other investment company, we are *built to create wealth* only for our clients—not for outside owners. That motivates us to *keep costs low*—currently less than one-fifth the industry average. This helps our fund investors to seek better earnings over time.

We are stewards of the assets of more than 20 million clients. With offices around the world we serve:

Individuals investing on their own.
Participants in employer-sponsored retirement plans.
Financial advisors.

The Money Machine of the 1%

Institutional investors.

Investors outside the United States.[18]

No matter which giant corporation we look at, Vanguard owns the highest shares in it.

Vanguard's Ownership of Shares in Major Corporations[19]

Company	Value of Shares ($1,000s)	Change in Value ($1,000s)	Change (%)	Shares Held
Apple, Inc.	3,02,42,730	-5,96,557	(1.93)	32,29,68,066
Microsoft Corp.	2,45,62,846	10,48,513	4.46	48,53,35,822
Exxon Mobil Corp.	2,33,47,894	4,97,351	2.18	26,19,53,264
Johnson & Johnson	1,97,75,571	4,14,993	2.14	17,53,93,093
General Electric Co.	1,70,42,195	-7,25,248	(4.08)	55,17,05,886
Facebook, Inc.	1,54,58,036	5,07,463	3.39	13,03,70,552
Amazon. Com, Inc.	1,50,52,087	4,18,924	2.86	2,20,10,802
Berkshire Hathaway, Inc.	1,45,07,552	3,66,781	2.59	9,87,64,735
AT&T, Inc.	1,40,29,589	3,14,841	2.30	35,88,13,013
Procter & Gamble Co.	1,39,44,831	3,48,792	2.57	17,22,22,198
Wells Fargo & Co.	1,38,93,080	2,47,574	1.81	27,46,21,069
JP Morgan Chase & Co.	1,38,75,209	2,66,636	1.96	21,75,13,853
Alphabet, Inc.	1,23,28,470	3,98,867	3.34	1,72,56,856
Verizon Communications, Inc.	1,22,98,730	2,96,279	2.47	23,96,47,897
Alphabet, Inc.	1,22,13,378	3,69,313	3.12	1,74,92,413
Chevron Corp.	1,22,09,953	3,20,205	2.69	11,81,87,525
Pfizer, Inc.	1,20,58,983	2,72,069	2.31	36,76,51,919
Coca-Cola Co.	1,17,86,160	2,83,303	2.46	26,20,31,119
Home Depot, Inc.	1,00,33,299	90,890	0.91	7,37,47,144
Pepsico, Inc.	97,89,526	57,398	0.59	9,46,48,806

Endnotes

[1] 'An Economy for the 1%: How Privilege and Power in the Economy Drive Extreme Inequality and How This Can Be Stopped'.Oxford: Oxfam, January 18, 2016. https://www.oxfam.org/sites/www.oxfam.org/files/file_attachments/bp210-economy-one-percent-tax-havens-180116-en_0.pdf.

[2] 'World's eight richest people have same wealth as poorest 50%', *The Guardian*. https://www.theguardian.com/global-development/2017/jan/16/worlds-eight-richest-people-have-same-wealth-as-poorest-50. Published on January 16, 2017; 'Just 8 men own same wealth as half the world', Oxfam International. https://www.oxfam.org/en/pressroom/pressreleases/2017-01-16/just-8-men-own-same-wealth-half-world. Published on January 16, 2017.

[3] Thomas Piketty and Emmanuel Saez, 'Income and Wealth Inequality: Evidence and Policy Implications'. October 2014. https://eml.berkeley.edu/_saez/lecture_saez_chicago14.pdf.

[4] Forbes World's Billionaires List in 'Just 8 men own same wealth as half the world', Oxfam International, 2017. http://www.oxfam.org/en/pressroom/pressreleases/2017-01-16/just-8-men-own-same-wealth-half-world.

[5] Eric Briys and Francois de Varenne, *The Fisherman and the Rhinoceros: How International Finance Shapes Everyday Life*. New Jersey: Wiley, 2000.

[6] Justin Podur, 'The Financial Economy and Real Economy', *Counter Punch*. http://www.counterpunch.org/2008/10/15/the-financial-economy-and-real-economy/. Published on October 15, 2008.

[7] For more on digital agriculture, see 'Digitised and Globalised Farming: What the Future Holds', in Susan Hawthorne, *Wild Politics: Feminism, Globalisation and Bio/diversity*. Victoria: Spinifex Press, 2002, pp. 236-249.

[8] Joel Kurtzman, quoted in Christopher Houghton Budd, *Finance at the Threshold: Rethinking the Real and Financial Economies*. New York: Routledge, 2016.

[9] The Gramm-Leach-Bliley Act (GLBA), also known as the Financial Services Modernization Act of 1999, is an act of the 106th United States Congress (1999–2001). It replaced the Glass–Steagall Act of 1933, removing market barriers for banking companies, securities companies and insurance companies.

[10] https://en.wikipedia.org/wiki/History_of_banking.

[11] John Summa, 'Do Option Sellers Have a Trading Edge?', *Investopedia*.

The Money Machine of the 1%

https://www.investopedia.com/articles/optioninvestor/03/100103.asp.

[12] Andy Crowder, 'Warren Buffett's Approach to Selling Puts', *Wyatt Investment Research*. http://www.wyattresearch.com/article/warren-buffett-approach-to-selling-puts/. Published on March 7, 2017.

[13] Alex Cripen,'CNBC Transcript: Warren Buffett Explains His Railroad "All-In Bet" on America', *CNBC*. https://www.cnbc.com/id/33603477. Published on November 3, 2009; Scott Patterson and Douglas A. Blackmon, 'Buffett Bets Big on Railroad', *The Wall Street Journal*. https://www.wsj.com/articles/SB10001424052748703740004574513191915147218. Updated on November 4, 2009.

[14] 'Victoria Nuland's assistant arrested—Fake Billions', *Justice4Poland.com*. https://justice4poland.com/2016/10/13/victoria-nulands-assistant-arrested-fake-billions/comment-page-1/. Published on October 13, 2016.

[15] 'Vanguard Group owns Monsanto-Academi Blackwater', https://edwardmd.wordpress.com/tag/vanguard-group-owns-monsanto-academi-blackwater/. Published on August 29, 2014; see also, www.academi.com.

[16] Landon Thomas Jr., 'Vanguard Is Growing Faster Than Everybody Else Combined', *The New York Times*. https://www.nytimes.com/2017/04/14/business/mutfund/vanguard-mutual-index-funds-growth.html. Published on April 14, 2017; http://en.wikipedia.org/wiki/The-Vanguard-Group.

[17] https://about.vanguard.com/; https://en.wikipedia.org/wiki/The_Vanguard_Group.

[18] www://vanguard.com/bogle_site/sp2004wellingtonbth.html.

[19] The figures for 'Vanguard's Ownership of Shares in Major Corporations' have been compiled through searches on various Internet databases on corporate shareholding in 2016. Since then, such searches have been blocked.

3 The Technology Machine of the 1%

How the Robber Barons and the Toxic Cartel poisoned our daily bread and the planet

OUR beautiful planet has evolved over 4-5 billion years and sustained humanity for 200,000 years. We have farmed for 10,000 years without toxins and poisons. We have eaten more than 10,000 species of plants, bred with intelligence for diversity, nutrition, taste, quality, and resilience. Today, the earth, our farms, our daily bread is poisoned and polluted, threatening the well-being of the planet and its inhabitants. Biodiversity is being pirated and plundered and pushed to extinction at a pace that threatens the very existence of our species. To quote Rosemary A. Mason, 'An anthropogenic mass extinction is underway that will affect all life on the planet and humans will struggle to survive the phenomenon'.[1]

Industrial agriculture, based on toxics and fossil fuels, is the main driver of both the sixth mass extinction and of climate change. High cost chemical farming has trapped farmers in debt, emptying out the countryside. More than 3,00,000 Indian farmers have committed suicide because of indebtedness.[2] According to a report submitted to the UN Human Rights Council by Hilal Elver, Special Rapporteur on Right to Food, and Baskut Tuncak, Special Rapporteur on Toxics, pesticides have 'catastrophic impacts on the environment, human health and society as a whole, including an estimated 2,00,000 deaths a year from acute poisoning...Chronic exposure to pesticides has been linked to cancer, Alzheimer's and Parkinson's diseases, hormone disruption, developmental disorders and sterility.'[3] Anthropogenic species extinction and climate change is ecocide, crimes against nature. Killing farmers through debt, and people through cancer and pesticide poisoning is genocide, crimes against humanity.

A century ago, the money and oil of the Robber Barons came together with the finances and toxic technologies from the labs of IG Farben to form the Toxic Cartel that evolved the tools of killing. This is how a century of ecocide and genocide through poisons and toxic chemicals began. Chemicals developed to kill people in Hitler's concentration camps during WWII became the agrichemicals for industrial agriculture when the war ended. This industrial agriculture was then forced on people everywhere.

Standard Oil and IG Farben founded a company, Standard IG Farben in 1927, and they exchanged patents to control economies on both sides of the Atlantic.[4] They joined hands to open up the Auschwitz concentration camp to produce artificial rubber and synthetic gasoline from coal. They provided the capital and technologies, while Hitler provided the labour of the concentration camp.[5]

Monsanto and Bayer, who are now merging, have a long history. They made explosives and lethally poisonous gases using shared technologies and sold them to both sides, the Allied and the Axis Powers, during the world wars. Bayer was then a part of IG Farben, Hitler's economic power and pre-war Germany's highest foreign exchange earner, with offices in the United States and Switzerland. IG Farben was also a foreign intelligence operation. Hermann Schmitz was the President of the company, his nephew Max Ilgner a director, while Ilgner's brother, Rudolph, handled the New York arm of the VOWI Network, as Vice President of Chemnyco. VOWI was a Nazi foreign intelligence operation.[6] Chemnyco was supported by a retainer fee from IG Farben and it handled the U.S. expenses of the company.[7] The American company was controlled by IG Farben and was a valuable source of information. It was investigated by the U.S. Department of Justice during the war.[8]

Paul Warburg, the brother of Max Warburg, a member of Farben Aufsichtsrat (supervisory board), founded the Federal Reserve System in the United States. The central banking system was created on December 23, 1918, with the enactment of the Federal Reserve Act. Warburg, in 1907, had published, 'A plan for a Modified Central Bank' in *The New York Times Financial Review*, which contributed to the creation of the Federal Reserve System.[9] Max Warburg and Hermann Schmitz were the central players in the Farben empire. Other 'guiding hands' of the FarbenVorstand (executive board) included Carl Bosch, Fritz ter Meer, Kurt Oppenheim and Georg von Schnitzler; each one of them was declared a war criminal after World War II, with the exception of Paul Warburg.

Monsanto and Bayer had a joint venture, MOBAY, in 1954 that was part of the Toxic Cartel of IG Farben. Controlling stakes in both corporations were with the same private equity firms. Their expertise was acquired in the arena of war. Monsanto entered into a partnership with IG Farben, Hitler's supplier of Zyklon-B, a cyanide based pesticide used in concentration camps during the Holocaust; it was used as evidence in the Nuremberg trials, which found Farben and its partners, which included Bayer, BASF and Hoechst (Aventis), guilty of war crimes.[10]

MOBAY supplied the ingredients for Agent Orange during the Vietnam War (1961-71), too; 20 million gallons of MOBAY defoliants and herbicides were sprayed over South Vietnam.[11] Monsanto and Bayer's cross-licensed Agent Orange resistance has also been cross-developed for decades. While wars were fought, lives were lost, and countries were carved into holy lands—with artificial boundaries that suit colonisation and resource grab—the two corporations sold chemicals as bombs and poisons.

The Toxic Cartel of the war has come together, once again. The Big 6 pesticide and GMO corporations that own the world's seed, pesticide and biotechnology industries are BASF, Bayer, Dupont, Dow Chemical Company, Monsanto, and Syngenta. Monsanto tried to buy Syngenta which is now merging with ChemChina; ChemChina's acquired Syngenta for US$ 43 billion and plans a merger with Sinochem in 2018. Dow Chemical which bought up Union Carbide (responsible for the Bhopal gas leak disaster that continues to kill and maim millions), is now merging with Dupont in a $130 billion deal. Not to be outdone, Bayer is buying up Monsanto for $66 billion. These deals alone will place as much as 70 per cent of the agrochemical industry in the world in the hands of only three merged companies. Through cross licensing agreements, who will be in the cockpit will be decided by issues like image-building, shedding liability, reducing taxes and expanding monopoly rights through patents on non-inventions.

According to Monsanto's website, Bayer CropScience AG and Monsanto have 'entered into a series of long-term business and licensing agreements related to key enabling agricultural technologies'. This gives Monsanto and Bayer free access to each other's herbicide and their paired herbicide-resistance technology. Through mergers and acquisitions, the biotech industry has become the IG Farben of today, with Monsanto in the cockpit. The latter's attempted buy-out of Syngenta would have merely been an accounting and liability reduction exercise within the much larger conglomerate of industrial chemical agriculture and biotechnology. There is no competition between

Big Agriculture and Biotech Corporations. In India, even the distribution channels for chemicals and seeds, and for the credit that farmers need to buy these toxins, are the same for Bayer and Monsanto.

The biotech industry—the chemical-military-industrial complex of our times—is a singular global entity. They have no concern for what happens to the farmers' crops once they have sold them their seeds and chemicals—unless, of course, the farmer hasn't used their seeds but the seeds have nevertheless managed to pollute the farm—then they sue the farmer! Such was the case with Australian organic farmer, Steve Marsh, whose field was contaminated by his neighbour's GM canola (mustard family but lacking the medicinal properties of mustard). The neighbour was later found to have been paid off by Monsanto.

While the different corporations that came out of the war years are presented as separate, they are one in terms of past and present partnerships, and their common ownership. Their biggest investors are the new financial giants, with the Vanguard Group in the lead (*see graphic and appendix on ownership of the Toxic Cartel on p. 59 and p. 60*).

The mergers are more like musical chairs, organised by the real owners, investment funds like Vanguard, Blackrock, Capital group, Fidelity, State Street Global Advisors, Norges Bank Investment Management (NBIM), and others. This game of musical chairs has two objectives—to expand markets and shrink liability. With a superficial merger, Monsanto, for instance, becomes a European company, sheds its name, and with it its liabilities, even as the cost of its damage to the earth and to communities become more visible. The 2016 Monsanto Tribunal and People's Assembly has made this shedding of liability and of the name Monsanto, an imperative. While

The Technology Machine of the 1%

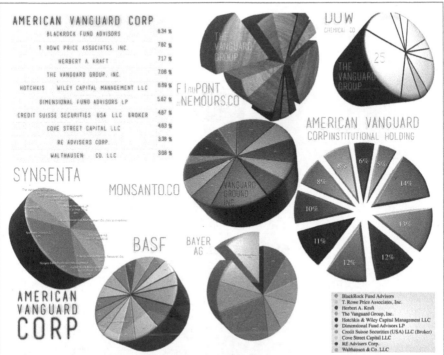

AMERICAN VANGUARD CORP

BLACKROCK FUND ADVISORS	6.34 %
T. ROWE PRICE ASSOCIATES, INC.	7.82 %
HERBERT A. KRAFT	7.17 %
THE VANGUARD GROUP, INC.	7.06 %
HOTCHKIS WILEY CAPITAL MANAGEMENT LLC	6.89 %
DIMENSIONAL FUND ADVISORS LP	5.82 %
CREDIT SUISSE SECURITIES USA LLC BROKER	4.87 %
COVE STREET CAPITAL LLC	4.63 %
RE ADVISERS CORP.	3.38 %
WALTHAUSEN CO. LLC	3.06 %

DUW CHEMICAL CO.

THE VANGUARD GROUP

25

THE VANGUARD GROUP

FI DuPONT NEMOURS.CO

AMERICAN VANGUARD CORP INSTITUTIONAL HOLDING

SYNGENTA

MONSANTO.CO

VANGUARD GROUND INC

8% 6% 5%
8% 14%
10% 13%
11% 12%
12%

BASF BAYER AG

AMERICAN VANGUARD CORP

- BlackRock Fund Advisors
- T. Rowe Price Associates, Inc.
- Herbert A. Kraft
- The Vanguard Group, Inc.
- Hotchkis & Wiley Capital Management LLC
- Dimensional Fund Advisors LP
- Credit Suisse Securities (USA) LLC (Broker)
- Cove Street Capital LLC
- RE Advisers Corp.
- Walthausen & Co. LLC

"Ron Lieber, a money-focused columnist with the New York Times whom I've mentioned here often, assembled a financial plan for investors who are completely fed up with the stock market. It's a plan that, as much as possible, avoids not only investing in the stock market but working with companies that trade on the stock market. I wrote about mutual insurance companies and how they might offer a benefit to policyholders over public companies, and that same structure exists for investment companies. Evan from My Journey to Millions pointed out that Vanguard is the investment equivalent of a mutual insurance company. Vanguard is not traded on the stock market, it is owned by its mutual funds, and therefore by all the investors in its mutual funds. The company's profits are used to return dividends to its investors and to lower management fees.

When owners and investors are the same, companies can't take advantage of one group to benefit another. That's the benefit in theory, but whether it is true in actuality is something that would need to be studied. Regardless, it may give investors a better feeling about the company with which they are investing. For that reason, Lieber recommends investing with Vanguard, USAA, or TIAA-CREF. Vanguard and USAA also offer ordinary retail banking as well, so you can replace your for-profit, fee-raising Wells Fargo or Bank of America with these customer-owned companies for a Wall Street-free banking experience."

Toxic Cartel.Toxic Capital.

The Vanguard Group, Inc.
Norges Bank Investment Management
Northern Cross LLC
Jupiter Asset Management Ltd.
Fidelity Management & Research Co.
UBS AG (Investment Management)
Artisan Partners LP
Credit Suisse AG
Capital Research & Management Co. (World Investors)
Syngenta AG

The Vanguard Group, Inc.
Norges Bank Investment Management
Northern Cross LLC
Fidelity Management & Research Co.
Capital Research & Management Co. (Global Investors)
Jupiter Asset Management Ltd.
UBS AG (Investment Management)
Artisan Partners LP
Credit Suisse AG
Capital Research & Management Co. (World Investors)
as of 31 Dec 2015

Capital Research & Management Co. (World Investors)
The Vanguard Group, Inc.
Lyxor International Asset Management SAS
Norges Bank Investment Management
State Street Global Advisors Ltd.
BlackRock Fund Advisors
Massachusetts Financial Services Co.
BlackRock Asset Management Deutschland AG
Amundi Asset Management SA (Investment Management)
Dodge & Cox

Capital Research & Management Co. (World Investors)
The Vanguard Group, Inc.
SSgA Funds Management, Inc.
BlackRock Fund Advisors
Tran Fund Management LP
T. Rowe Price Associates, Inc.
Highfields Capital Management LP
Northern Trust Investments, Inc.
DuPont Capital Management Corp.

The Vanguard Group, Inc.
SSgA Funds Management, Inc.
BlackRock Fund Advisors
Capital Research & Management Co. (World Investors)
Third Point LLC
Capital Research & Management Co. (Global Investors)
Wellington Management Co. LLP
Northern Trust Investments, Inc.
Capital Research & Management Co. (International Investors)
Franklin Advisors, Inc.

Capital Research & Management Co. (Global Investors)
The Vanguard Group, Inc.
SSgA Funds Management, Inc.
BlackRock Fund Advisors
Massachusetts Financial Services Co.
Glenview Capital Management LLC
Fidelity Management & Research Co.
Sende Capital Management LLC
PRIMECAP Management Co.
Davis Selected Advisers LP

MONOPOLY

NAVDANYA

ostensibly shutting down its troublesome products like Roundup, Monsanto can simultaneously expand its market in Europe as a European company; the buyout will even be financed by European taxpayers, without their permission or knowledge.[12] The Monsanto Tribunal was jointly organised by movements and institutions from across the world from October 14-16, 2016, in The Hague to hold the Toxic Cartel accountable for a century of crimes against nature and humanity, the crimes of ecocide and genocide.[13]

In two decades of R&D, countless mergers and acquisitions, and billions of dollars spent on lobbying, the seed industry has given us precisely three traits. One was Terminator, declared illegal in the late 1990s; the other two are Herbicide Tolerance and Bt-Toxin.

On March 25, 2016, the Competition Commission of India (CCI) blocked the Monsanto-Bayer merger. The global level deal had been under CCI scrutiny amid apprehensions about the possible adverse impact on the genetically modified market competition in the country. Bayer appealed the rejection, and the merger was opened up to the public for comments and objections in January 2018. (The CCI launches a public consultation process if it is of the 'prima facie opinion that a combination has, or is likely to have an appreciable adverse effect on competition'.) I made an objection on January 21, 2018. The details of the merger, along with my objections, are available on my website, *vandanashiva.com*, under 'Monsanto-Bayer "Combination"—Comments Submitted to the Competition Commission of India'. While this was an important step, we need to continue building movements to prevent the ever increasing corporate control over our seeds and our daily bread by strengthening Bija Swaraj and Anna Swaraj, and continuing the Bija Satyagraha.

Corporations like Monsanto, Bayer, Dow, Dupont, and Syngenta, through free trade, neoliberal polices and the deregulation of commerce, are enlarging their empire with mega buyouts. Such is the case with the most recent bid by Bayer to buy Monsanto, facilitated by the European Central Bank. This, in effect, means public money is being used to strengthen the monopoly of those who destroy life and people's rights. The European Union cleared the Monsanto-Bayer merger on March 21, 2018, 'conditional on the divestiture of an extensive remedy package, which addresses the parties' overlaps in seeds, pesticides and digital agriculture'.[14]

Across the world people are rising, and democratic governments are responding to stop this ecocide and genocide. In addition to the global Monsanto Tribunal, a People's Assembly on Dow Dupont was organised by Navdanya in Bhopal on November 29, 2016.[15] In April 2017, another People's Assembly on the Bayer-Monsanto merger was held during the Annual General Body meeting of Bayer in Cologne.[16] These giant corporations have responded by attacking the laws and policies of governments that take action in response to people's movements and the call to protect the earth as well as people's rights. One of the now many examples of this is of Bayer suing the Indian government in order to retain its monopoly rights on its hazardous drug, Nexavar.[17]

Today, not only is the old Toxic Cartel recombining as a new one through mega mergers, it is going beyond the convergence of seeds, pesticides, and chemical fertilisers, to farm equipment and information technologies, and to climate data, soil data, and insurance, in a bid to have total control over our daily food. This is a ruthless takeover by the violent paradigm of profit at any cost. And even while science is abused and truth is violated, these war-based corporations use the word 'science' (not the practise) to expand their toxic empire on the basis of a public relations spin: that without poisons and the Toxic Cartel, the world will starve.

A failed strategy continues to be offered as the future because it is central to the linear narrative of 'progress' and 'control', and of 'technology' as defined by the 1%. This is the basis of their imposing false narratives of being 'creators', and of carrying out the civilising mission of our times—making profits through increased risk and vulnerability in times of ecological and social collapse. This is also the basis of claiming patents on life, with the 1% masquerading as 'inventors' and 'creators'. For them, patents, revenue collections and monopolies are the end game.

Information technology and biotechnology are integrating in a new 'green' gold rush, with Bill Gates and Monsanto in the lead. IT is being used to 'mine' genetic data and claim patents on plants that neither Gates nor Monsanto created, and about which they have no knowledge—they only have 'data'.

The climate crisis, to which industrialised, fossil fuel-based agriculture contributes 50 per cent, is now being used by Gates to launch new rogue ventures for geoengineering. Monsanto is using technology to pirate climate resilient seeds that farmers have bred, turn climate data and soil data into new commodities for new monopolies, and link them to insurance. The company sees a $3 trillion market in agriculture with the convergence of data, insurance, seeds and chemicals.[18]

Owning our seeds through seed freedom, our own food through food freedom, our own minds and intelligence through intellectual freedom, our own economies through freedom to produce and consume ecologically and locally, is the 'barbarianism' that the 1% would like to extinguish. These are the freedoms that I, and diverse social movements, are committed to defending.

Genetic determinism, genetic reductionism, and genetic engineering

Genetic determinism and genetic reductionism are an attempt to force life itself into a mechanical mould; they are not a natural evolution of society's intellectual search for understanding the world, of which we are a part. Rather, they are a political project of domination and control. The genetic engineering paradigm did not evolve; it was artificially constructed by the big money of Rockefeller, the richest man of his time.

The term 'molecular biology' was coined in 1938 by Warren Weaver of the Rockefeller Foundation. From 1932 to 1959, $25 million was poured into molecular biology programmes in the US, a quarter of the Foundation's total spending. The groundwork for genetic engineering was created with funding from the Rockefeller Foundation, with the profits made by Standard Oil. Today, the Bill and Melinda Gates Foundation is playing that same role.

As Lily Kay reports in *The Molecular Vision of Life*, molecular biology was aimed at 'restructuring human relations in congruence with the social framework of industrial capitalism'.[19] Originally, the discipline was called social psychology, and was a 'science' of social control, based on 'conditioned power'. In the social construct of the 'gene' as a physiological site of social control, 'the goal of selective breeding as a corrective to the perceived swapping and degeneration of the Anglo Saxon stock acquired a precise target'.[20]

Eugenics was an important part of the project of the construction of the 'gene'. For the Rockefeller Foundation, which drove the project, it was important 'to restrict the breeding of the feeble minded... [and] social dysfunction due to society's inability to adapt to the dislocations of technological change. These problems would be addressed through social control'.[21] Instead of adapting tools and technology to the needs of people and society, society would be manipulated to adapt to these tools. The roots of today's genetic engineering lie in the human engineering, the genetic reductionism and genetic determinism of the 1930s.

Then, as now, the issue is control. Then, as now, the prejudice of the super rich, and their fear of women, the poor, the migrant, and the coloured, shapes what they call 'science', as the ultimate objective truth, when in reality it is the articulation of subjective prejudice, of fear of the other, of the uncontrollable urge to dominate.

During the dozen or so years following 1953, all but one of the Nobel Prizes—in Physiology or Medicine—was awarded for research sponsored by the Rockefeller Foundation.[22] It is, therefore, not surprising that as the project of genetic engineering, based on an artificial science and false assumptions of how life works, starts to fail no fewer than 107 Nobel Laureates have been mobilised to defend a genetic engineering product, Golden Rice, which has failed to deliver in two decades. A letter of support was issued on June 29, 2016, to Greenpeace and other groups actively campaigning against the use of GM crops. As of July 2018, the number of signatories to this letter is 134.

The genetic engineering paradigm invades life itself, redefining people and living organisms as machines to be manipulated and engineered. Defining a construct, the 'gene', as the building block of life, is scientifically flawed. As Richard Lewontin has said in *The Doctrine of DNA*,

> DNA is a dead molecule, among the most non-reactive, chemically inert molecules in the world. It has no power to reproduce itself. Rather, it is produced out of elementary materials by a complex cellular machinery of proteins. While it is often said that DNA produces proteins, in fact proteins (enzymes) produce DNA.
>
> When we refer to genes as self-replicating, we endow them with a mysterious autonomous power that seems to place them above the more ordinary materials of the body. Yet, if anything in the world can be said to be self-replicating it is not the gene, but the entire organism as a complex system.[23]

Genetic reductionism is the basis of genetic engineering and GMOs which were promoted by the Toxic Cartel as the miracle tools for transforming agriculture. We need to heed the caution of Carl R. Woese, one of the most important microbiologists of our times,

> Society cannot tolerate a biology whose metaphysical base is outmoded and misleading: society desperately needs to live in harmony with the rest of the living world, not with a biology that is a distorted and [an] incomplete reflection of that world. Because it has been taught to accept the above hierarchy of the sciences, society today perceives biology as here to solve its problems, to change the living world...society will come to see that biology is here to understand the world, not primarily to change it. Biology's primary job is to teach us. In that realization lies our hope of learning to live in harmony with our planet.[24]

Genetic determinism and reductionism go hand in hand, but to say that genes are primary is more ideology than science. Genes are not independent entities, but dependent parts of an entirety that gives them effect. All parts of the cell interact, and the combinations of genes are at least as important as their individual effects in the making of an organism. More broadly, an organism cannot be treated simply as the product of a number of proteins, each produced by the corresponding gene. Genes have multiple effects, and most traits depend on multiple genes. Yet, the linear and reductionist causality of genetic determinism is held onto, even though the very processes that make genetic engineering possible run counter to the concepts of 'master molecules' and the 'central dogma'.

Genetic engineering has epistemological and ethical implications for the material conditions of our life, our health, and our environment: it moves genes across species by using 'vectors'—usually a mosaic recombination of natural genetic parasites from different sources, including viruses causing cancers and other diseases in animals and plants that are tagged with one or more antibiotic resistant 'marker' genes. Evidence accumulated over the past few years confirms the fear that these vectors constitute major sources of genetic pollution with drastic ecological and public health consequences. Vector-mediated horizontal gene transfer and recombinations are found to be involved in generating new pandemic strains of bacterial pathogens.

Biotech technicians do not have either the scientific expertise of gene ecology or that of the multiple disciplines needed for the risk assessment of GMOs in the context of the environment and public health.

Deeper and ethical scientific research has led to the emergent field of epigenetics. While genetic reductionism leads to the false assumption that genes control the traits of life, the new science of epigenetic control reveals that life is controlled by something over and above the genes. Environmental signals acting through membrane switches control gene activity. Environmentally derived signals activate membrane switches that send secondary signals into the cell nucleus, and within the nucleus the signals select gene blueprints and control the manufacture of specific proteins. Epigenetic mechanisms can edit the read-out of a gene so as to create over 30,000 different variations of proteins for the same gene blueprint. Epigenetics describes how gene activity and cellular expression are regulated by information from the environment, and not via the internal matter of DNA.

The limitation at a higher systems level is even more serious. For example, Bt brinjal is being offered as a pest control solution; a gene for producing a toxin is being inserted into the plant, along with antibiotic resistance markers and viral promoters. This is like using a JCB (earth-moving equipment) to make a hole in the wall of your house for putting up a painting. Just as the JCB will destroy the wall, the transgenic transformation will disrupt the metabolism and the self-regulatory processes of the organism. Genetic engineering is 'high tech', like the JCB, but it is also crude tech for the sensitive task of maintaining the ecological fabric of agriculture to control pests. Pests are controlled through biodiversity, through organic practices which build up resilience to pests and disease. In Navdanya, we do not use pesticides and have no pests; in Andhra Pradesh, a government project for non-pesticide management has successfully covered 14 lakh acres so far.

The scientific alternative to the crude tech of putting

toxic genes into our food is agroecology. Based on a global survey of peer reviewed studies, the International Assessment of Agricultural Science and Technology for Development (IAASTD) has recognised that agroecology-based systems outperform farming systems that use genetic engineering. Epigenetics and agroecology are the sciences for the future. Reductionist biology is a primitive science of the past.

Peddling poisons and scientific fraud, stealing lives

Ever since Monsanto came to India over two decades ago with its GMO Bt (*Bacillus thuringiensis*) cotton, it has broken several laws, deceived farmers by making unscientific and fraudulent claims, raked in huge profits collecting illegal royalties by violating India's patent and intellectual property laws, and forced farmers into deep debt, resulting in suicides. Farmers are also dying of pesticide poisoning as Bt cotton requires excessive pesticide use to control bollworms and other new 'super pests' that have emerged due to the failure of Bt cotton's supposed pest control technology.

Monsanto introduced Bt cotton illegally in the country in 1995. In India, GMOs are regulated by the Rules for the Manufacture, Use, Import, Export and Storage of Hazardous Micro Organisms, Genetically Engineered Organisms or Cells, 1989, framed under the Environment (Protection) Act, 1986. On March 10, 1995, Mahyco, Monsanto's local collaborator, imported 100 grams of Bt cotton seed after obtaining permission from the Review Committee of Genetic Manipulation (RCGM), under the Department of Biotechnology, and not from the Ministry of Environment, Forest and Climate Change's Genetic Engineering Approval Committee (GEAC), the only body that can grant permission for importing genetically engineered substances (seeds in the this case), and give approvals for field trials and a commercial release.

In 1998, Mahyco-Monsanto began large scale, multi-centric, open field trials over 40 acres in 40 locations, spread across nine states.[25] These field trials, too, were undertaken without permission from the GEAC.

The GEAC clearance for commercial planting of Bt cotton finally came in 2002 on the grounds that Bt cotton had pest control technology for the bollworm. Peddling this fraudulent claim, the company established a seed monopoly, even though patenting seeds is forbidden in India under Articles 3(H) and 3(J) of The Patents Act, 1970. Monsanto knew that its actions would lead to farmers incurring massive debts, but even when the epidemic of farmers' suicides started in Maharashtra— nearly 85 per cent of the more than 3,00,000 farmers' suicides have happened in this cotton growing region where Monsanto has established a 99 per cent seed monopoly[26]—the company simply continued with its plundering policies. In fact, since the legalisation of Bt cotton, Monsanto has made Rs 7,000 crore through collection of royalty from farmers, reports *Outlook* (March 2017).

High seed prices and seed monopoly have been challenged through several cases. On August 30, 2005, a farmer's collective in Andhra Pradesh, Ryotu Sangham, had made a representation before the erstwhile Monopolies and Restrictive Trade Practices Commission (MRTPC), now the Competition Commission of India (CCI). The state government joined the case, and we also intervened. The MRTPC observed that Mahyco-Monsanto Biotech (India) Private Limited (MMBL) was indeed in a position to charge arbitrarily for the Bt cotton technology and could not

offer any rational explanation for arriving at the trait value of
Rs 1,250 per packet. The MRTPC, vide its interim order dated
May 11, 2006, stated,'There is a basic difference between royalty
and trait value...and (these) are not synonymous... In any case,
the lump sum payment of Rs 50 lakhs may be considered as
royalty for the same, but the future payments on sale cannot be
termed as royalty'. It also held that '...by temporary injunction
the MMBL is directed during the pendency of this case not
to charge trait value of Rs 900 for a packet of 450 gms of Bt
cotton seed and to fix a reasonable trait value'.

In 2015, the Government of India initiated a case in the CCI
challenging Monsanto's monopoly in the cotton seed sector
(Case No. 02/2015 & Case No 107/2015). The CCI observed
that there was prima facie evidence of monopoly and started an
investigation. It found that the company was imposing excessive
trait fee and adding unfair clauses in the sub-license agreements
leading to a monopoly. Monsanto immediately went to the Delhi
High Court (Case No: WP [C] 1776 of 2016) challenging the
CCI's price regulation as well as Article 3(J) of The Patent Act,
which excludes seeds, plants and animals from patenting.

Fourteen years after the commercialisation of Bt cotton,
the Indian government accepted that the GMO variety has
essentially failed. In an affidavit filed on January 23, 2016, in
the Delhi High Court, it has stated:

> Pink bollworm, a major pest to the cotton crop, has already
> developed resistance in the last 2-3 years; farmers are a worried
> lot having sown Bt cotton seeds purchased at high price.... The
> crop is getting damaged due to pink bollworm incidence. It is
> a natural phenomenon that over the years, [the] efficacy of the
> technology goes down, hence the royalty on technology should also
> be reduced. ... cotton seeds are now unaffordable to farmers due

to high royalties charged by MMBL (Mahyco-Monsanto Biotech Ltd.) which has a near monopoly on Bt cotton seeds and that this has led to a market failure.

That the bollworm has developed a resistance to the Bt toxin was known in 2002, and more scientific evidence establishing this fact has been collected since then.[27]

For cotton, the emergence of Bt resistant budworms and bollworms poses a real risk once this historically effective pest control agent loses its effectiveness. The Bt toxin is released in every cell and part of the plant making the pests resistant to Bt, and creating 'super pests', which require more pesticide use. Cotton farmers in the country have been forced to buy and use more pesticides as not only has Bt cotton failed to control the bollworm it has led to the emergence of new pests. The resultant debt has forced many to take their own lives.

Farmers are dying due to pesticide poisoning as well. According to Kishor Tiwari, Chair of the Vasantrao Naik Shetkari Swavalamban Mission (VNSSM), Maharashtra government's task force on agrarian distress, nine farmers died due to pesticide poisoning in Vidarbha in September 2017. Four others lost their vision and 70 are under treatment at the Vasantrao Naik Government Medical College and Hospital in Yavatmal after spraying the toxic insecticide.[28] The death toll increased to 35 in a few days, and the government charged the pesticide companies with culpable homicide.[29] Tiwari has clearly stated that in the case of pesticide poisoning deaths Monsanto is liable because it is the failure of its Bt cotton that led to pesticide use and the related deaths.

In October 2017, Maharashtra Chief Minister Devendra Fadnavis ordered a Special Investigation Team (SIT) probe, assuring that a case of culpable homicide will be registered against pesticide manufacturers for claiming that the pesticides would control pests. However, it is Monsanto which first claimed that its Bt cotton will control pests and negate the use of pesticides. So the probe for culpable homicide should begin with Monsanto.[30]

Monsanto's illegal spread of Roundup Ready Bt cotton

Even though Monsanto's Bt technology has failed miserably in India, the company has been pushing another toxic product, Roundup Ready (RR) Bt cotton, without commercial approvals. Roundup, a glyphosate-based herbicide, is a World Health Organisation (WHO) declared 'probable carcinogen'. RR Bt cotton, packaged as Bollgard-II, is illegal. In 2017, after reports of contamination, farmers in Vidarbha collected samples from different areas and sent them to the Nagpur-based Central Institute for Cotton Research (CICR) for testing. Bolls collected from six fields tested positive for Roundup Ready Flex, confirming the presence of RR Bt cotton, a major health hazard in countries where Roundup is promoted as a weed control technology and where Roundup Ready crops are widely used— in the U.S., thousands of cancer patients are suing Monsanto; in Europe, there is a strong movement to get Roundup banned.

Monsanto has been spreading RR Bt cotton in Vidarbha as well as Andhra Pradesh, another leading cotton-producing state, without the requisite permission. Although in October 2017, the government of Andhra Pradesh had ordered its officers to monitor the illegal spread of RR Bt cotton, the directive was suddenly withdrawn.[31]

Mahyco-Monsanto has deferred its application for seeking

approval from the GEAC for this variety, which was in the works since 2007. In its letter to the regulatory agency, the company, stating that Bt cotton has transformed the lives of Indian farmers, attacked India's Essential Commodities Act, the Seed Price Control Order, as well as the exclusions from patenting and royalty collection built into Article 3(J) of The Patents Act—all of which are aimed at protecting farmers' right to reliable and affordable seeds.

Illegal cultivation of RR Bt cotton needs the same response that illegal farming of Bt cotton had received in 2001 in Gujarat. When Navbharat Seeds, an Ahmedabad-based company, was found to be promoting the illegal cultivation of Bt cotton through its Navbharat 151 brand, it had prompted an unprecedented response from the GEAC, which had ordered the destruction of standing cotton crop at the time. The order was challenged by Navbharat in the Delhi High Court and the regulatory authority, in its submission to the court, had stated:

> The destruction of the cotton produce as well as seeds harvested from this plant is...necessary. The cotton which has been produced is genetically modified cotton, the effect of which, i.e., allergenicity and other factors on mammals are not tested. The precautionary principles would require that no product, the effect of which is unknown, be put into the market stream. This cotton which in appearance is no different from any other cotton will intermingle with ordinary cotton and it will become impossible to contain its adverse effect. The only remedy is to destroy the cotton as well as the seeds produced and harvested in this manner. Since the farmers are being put to a loss, the further process to determine the compensation payable to farmers, who have unwittingly used this product has to be determined and undertaken. I would respectfully

submit that every day of delay in this matter poses a threat to the environment. (*Excerpted from the GEAC Order*)

Roundup and the spread of cancer

There is global evidence that Roundup has led to the spread of disease, especially cancer. There are increasing demands for a ban on this carcinogen in Europe as well as in the US.[32] In fact, 45 per cent of soil in Europe has been found to be contaminated with Roundup.[33]

In spite of the fact that research by UN agencies as well as independent scientists has established that certain chemicals are carcinogenic, the industry continues to promote chemicals in farming. Monsanto launched a massive attack on WHO, that declared Roundup as a probable carcinogen, as it had done on other scientists whose research had shown that Roundup and Roundup Ready GMOs are contributing to cancer.

According to the medical journal, *The Lancet*, exposure to glyphosate has been shown to cause tumours of the mammary glands in rats. The International Agency for Research on Cancer, too, has linked glyphosate exposure to cancer. Roundup is several times more toxic than glyphosate alone.[34]

In the US, thousands of patients of non-Hodgkin lymphoma, a type of blood cancer, have sued Monsanto for personal injury and wrongful death due to exposure to the herbicide weed killer. More than 100 of those lawsuits have been consolidated in a multidistrict litigation in a federal court in San Francisco, California, while similar lawsuits are pending in state courts in Missouri, Delaware, Arizona and elsewhere.

The Monsanto Papers, a collection of documents which include internal emails, text messages, company reports, studies and other memoranda, obtained during pre-trial investigation, have exposed how the company knew Roundup is carcinogenic; how it attacked scientists who presented research confirming links between Roundup and cancer; and how it paid off scientists and journalists. The documents obtained via Discovery (civil procedure in the US allowing the parties to obtain evidence from each other) revealed that Monsanto runs an internal programme, Let Nothing Go, which employs an army of Internet trolls besides scientists and journalists. It has now been revealed how the company mounted a smear campaign against Gilles-Éric Séralini, the French scientist who published a groundbreaking study showing an increase in tumors among rats fed genetically modified corn and Monsanto's herbicide weed killer. Additionally, the 'draft' of an article written by Monsanto for *Forbes* 'journalist' Henry Miller in 2015, identical to the report that appeared with Miller's byline in the American business magazine, was found. *Forbes* has been forced to pull down the story and terminate Miller's employment.[35]

Brent Wisner, a lawyer at Baum Hedlund Aristei Goldman, the firm representing the cancer victims, said of the Monsanto Papers,

> This is a look behind the curtain. These show that Monsanto has deliberately been stopping studies that look bad for them, ghostwriting literature and engaging in a whole host of corporate malfeasance. They (Monsanto) have been telling everybody that these products are safe because regulators have said they are safe, but it turns out that Monsanto has been in bed with U.S. regulators while misleading European regulators.

Monsanto's influence on scientists and regulators has become a global problem.[36] Independent scientists and journalists have been systematically attacked to maintain the false propaganda that GMOs are the miracle panacea to feed the world and that GMOs, as an invention, justify patent monopolies. This has led to Monsanto media and Monsanto public relations being paraded as 'science' and governments being hijacked by corporations that continue to push GMOs despite scientific evidence to the contrary. Indeed, governments that make and enforce laws to protect their citizens, in accordance with international obligations to exclude patents on seed and on life, and to protect biodiversity and prevent biopiracy are facing major attacks from corporations like Monsanto. While competition is the rhetoric of free trade agreements, monopoly is the only outcome.

Climate change, big data and digital agriculture: the future of agriculture according to the 1%

There are three kinds of convergence taking place in agriculture. The first is the merger of corporations such as Monsanto and Bayer. The second is the takeover of mega corporations by the billionaires through their investment funds. The third is the merger of biotechnology and information technology.

In 2013, Monsanto acquired one of the world's largest climate data corporations, Climate Corporation, for $1 billion; and in 2014, it acquired the world's largest soil data corporation, Solum, Inc.[37] Both companies combine Monsanto's patented GMO seeds with propriety platforms which, like seeds, are a source of royalty and super profits.

Climate Corporation does not bring the farmer deeper insights about the role of industrial agriculture in contributing to climate instability. It does not share the knowledge that the solution to climate change lies below our feet, in the soil, and how recycling organic matter on the farm is the most effective mitigation and adaptation response to climate change. No. Climate Corporation sells 'data'. It's website states:

> The company's proprietary Climate Technology Platform™ combines hyper-local weather monitoring, agronomic modeling, and high-resolution weather simulations to deliver a suite of tools that helps farmers manage risk through precision agriculture products and services, including: precision farming equipment and software, prescriptive agriculture technologies, and insurance products. The company's Climate Basic™ and Climate Pro™ mobile SaaS solutions help farmers improve profitability by making better informed operating decisions.[38]

Solum, Inc. does not work with farmers to understand the rich soil food web—bacteria, fungi, earthworms.... 'The asset acquisition by Monsanto Company, the Climate Corporation's parent company, includes the Solum brand, soil testing intellectual property, the soil test lab in Ames, Iowa, and Solum's No-Wait Nitrate™ platform.' It continues to be the chemical and intellectual property treadmill which has destroyed the soil and is killing our farmers. The Climate Corporation recognises that farmers make hundreds of decisions daily, decisions that are voluntary, the autonomous decisions of a farmer who thinks and uses her own mind.

Monsanto has also collaborated with the world's three biggest farm equipment companies—Deere & Co, CNH Industrial, and AGCO—and is working with Deere to put 'spyware' into farm machinery in order to collect data on farms. It is buying IT firms not just to make farmers more dependent on them, but, increasingly, on surveillance. For Monsanto, data is not just another commodity, it is 'intelligence'.

The Technology Machine of the 1%

As John Hamer, managing director of Monsanto Growth Ventures (the venture capital arm of Monsanto which has acquired 12 Silicon Valley companies) says frankly, 'If you think about it, there are two people on earth that need to know a lot about remote sensing (technology)—Monsanto and the CIA.'[39] Hamer was referring to the use of technology, such as satellites and drones, for farm surveillance by providing a constant flow of images of what's happening on a given farm. Monsanto's Integral Farming Systems Platform has been set up by combining digital agriculture, data science and genetic engineering, creating higher level integrations of abstractions and instruments for control, which is not the basis of food security.

David Friedberg, who established Climate Corporation, which he then sold to Monsanto, has no idea that ecological farmers, through their rich experiential knowledge, offer the most significant and real response to climate change. That their real knowledge produces real food and real nourishment. He does not see farmers as producers of food, but as consumers of commodities, now also of 'climate data' that he will help Monsanto sell.[40]

What Climate Corporation, now Monsanto, is focused on is the global $3 trillion agriculture industry; it is also looking at markets created by the $400 billion subsidies for industrial agriculture, and government policies that help captive markets grow. For instance, the Corporation states that it serves as an authorised provider of the U.S. Federal Crop Insurance programme.

Friedberg, who thinks he can tell farmers what to grow and how to grow it on the basis of the massive data that he has collected from farmers and churned into 'big data' using propriety programmes, has no idea of the richness of biodiversity in the world.

The intelligence of microbes in the soil and in our gut is just beginning to be recognised by independent science, but this knowledge is already being cannibalised by the mechanical mind for the money machine. The National Microbiome Initiative (NMI) of the US government, in collaboration with the Gates Foundation, 'include[s] techniques that can analyze the entire genomes of specific microbes; track the movements of molecules between or within cells; and add, remove, edit, stimulate, or block specific species with precision. That will allow microbiologists to accurately simulate communities of microbes, predict how they will change over time, and then modify them accordingly'.[41]

The new robber barons and their digital empires

Bill Gates is the modern day Columbus. His empire is the continuation of colonisation five hundred years after the first colonisation. Columbus needed the Pope, a king, and a queen for the conquest of non-European, non-Christian societies, based on a civilising mission that would ensure 'the Catholic faith and the Christian religion be exalted and be everywhere increased and spread, that the health of souls be cared for and that barbarous nations be overthrown and brought to the faith itself'.[42] Today, the civilising mission of imposing the Christian religion on non-Christian cultures has given way to the civilising mission of forcing GMOs and digital dictatorship on small farmers and tiny businesses across the world. Bill Gates is the Pope of his religion of the worship and imposition of genetic engineering and digital tools. Those who live in pluralistic worlds of biodiversity and diverse agriculture, diverse economies, diverse technologies, diverse languages, and diverse intelligences are the new 'digital barbarians' who must be 'civilised' and brought into the empire of the 1%.

Technology is the process of creating the means to order and transform matter, energy, and information to realise ends which are at a higher level than the tools themselves. Tools, and technologies as tools, evolve according to need, and are assessed and used as means. They are not ends in themselves; they are chosen, not imposed.

In the fossil fuel age of industrial capitalism and in the age of 'digital data', data is being made the new oil, the new lubricant of the money machine. Technology is more than a tool now. It is an instrument of power and control, the means to construct a false narrative of our relationship with the natural world and society, eclipsing nature's creativity and productivity, and the contribution of those who are colonised—women, slaves, workers, and farmers. Besides narrowing the meaning of technology to violent industrial tools, technological fundamentalism inverts the means-end relationship. Instead of being a means to reaching higher ecological, ethical, social and human ends, the deployment and use of industrial technologies become an end in themselves, a new religion. Industrial agriculture and genetic engineering were elevated from a means to be assessed and chosen, to a religion to be imposed as civilising missions on 'barbarians' practicing ecological agriculture. Instead of being evaluated against other tools on ecological and social criteria, those calling for scientific assessments of technology are declared as 'anti-science'. Such a discourse comes from religious fundamentalism, not from rational scientific debate.

The reductionism associated with technology is also reflected in the reductions in society—the 99% lose their economic security; their diverse skills, ways of thinking, potentials, and intelligences are reduced to the management of digital data; and people end up as appendages to machines and technologies.

The 1% economy works against democracy. Over the last two decades of globalisation, we have seen that large areas of economic decision-making have moved out of the democratic control of people and parliaments. The rules of the game are written by the rich who own the corporations, enabling them to transfer larger parts of the economy into the hands of corporations. These powerful corporations then either bypass governments, or corrupt them, or buy democracy, as demonstrated in the Citizens United case in the US where the Supreme Court ruled in 2010 that corporate financing of elections constituted the 'freedom' of speech of corporations. In some cases, the 1% use their wealth to buy up institutions, shape global policy, and distort public priorities without any public accountability or democratic scrutiny. The very fact that the 1% can control the wealth of the 99% is an expression of the breakdown of economic democracy and justice.

We tell the story of the new colonisation by the 1% through the journey of Bill Gates who, in August 2017 had $89 billion in the bank, and has been the richest man in the world since 2013. In 2015, he was worth $81.6 billion which was nearly $6 billion more than the $76 billion he had in March 2014, and the $76 billion was $9 billion more than he was worth in March 2013. He is among the five men who control as much wealth as 50 per cent of humanity. Gates knows how to create and run the money machine.[43]

While presenting himself as a philanthropist who gives away his money, Gates has a personal investment company,

Cascade Investment LLC, funded solely by himself and run by Michael Larson, one of the most powerful men in US wealth management. Gates now has vast holdings in real estate and non-tech companies, like the Canadian National Railway Co.; AutoNation Inc., an American automotive retailer; and Republic Services Inc., a waste management company. He is making more money than he is giving away.[44]

We tell the story of Big Wealth and Big Money in our times by focusing on Gates and his role in destroying self-organsation in nature and society to engineer monopolies through mastery, conquest, invasion and dictatorship by the tools he owns and controls for rent collection, which in his double-speak, he calls 'innovation'.

While he has been central to the establishment of the new civilising mission of technology as a religion, Gates himelf did not invent anything. Microsoft Basic is based on BASIC (an acronym for Beginner's All-purpose Symbolic Instruction Code), designed in 1964 by John G. Kemeny and Thomas E. Kurtz at Dartmouth College (New Hampshire, USA) to make it easy for non-science, non-math students to use computers. Before the introduction of BASIC, computers required the writing of custom software which only scientists and mathematicians could do. Microsoft BASIC (MBASIC) became one of the leading applications in the world, but even the operating systems were developed by others.[45] Gates made his billions through patent monopolies, by enclosing the commons of software. The open source software movement began as a response to the patent monopoly; the free software movement is to patented propriety software what our seed freedom movement is to seeds.

Gates is now using his economic power to expand his patent empire to the living world, to enclose the biological and knowledge commons through patenting and biopiracy. He is trying to control the seed by controlling the gene banks where the biodiversity of the world is stored; he is trying to pirate and patent climate resilient crops evolved by farmers; he is trying to use digital tools to take genomic patents on biodiversity and agriculture; he is trying to enclose our food commons by imposing GMO foods. Not only is Gates propping up failed GMOs, he is pushing new GMOs which are known to not work. Notably, through the Cornell Alliance for Science he is promoting the failed GMO varities of Bt brinjal and Golden Rice.

Whereas with the bonus of tax free trade on software, the Microsoft monopoly went global, now, with DivSeek, CRISPR *(for details on the gene-editing and gene mapping techniques, see p. 98 and p. 101)* and the genetically engineered mosquitoes in Florida, Gates wants to control our food, our diversity and our heritage. And to top it all, he is financing a most unscientific and irresponsible experiment, that of geoengineering.

The vision of one agriculture, one science, one monoculture, one monopoly

Bill Gates who is pushing One Agriculture has partnered with the Mexican telecom magnate, Carlos Slim, to use smartphones to dumb down the farmer, as he waits for instructions from the machine and loses his capacity to know his farming, soil and seed.[46]

Similarly, Facebook's Mark Zuckerberg, has tried selling big data to farmers in India through Free Basics, essentially repackaged *internet.org*, which provides free basic Internet access to users in collaboration with telecom operators. It's a system through which Facebook decides what information is important for the users.

Zuckerberg brought Free Basics to India in partnership with Reliance Industries, an Indian mega-corporation with interests in telecom, energy, food, retail, infrastructure and land. Reliance has acquired land from the Indian government for setting up rural cell phone towers and also grabbed land from farmers for creating Special Economic Zones (SEZs). Consequently—and at no extra cost—it has a huge rural, semi-urban and suburban user base, especially farmers. Despite Zuckerberg deploying a whopping Rs 100 crore to advertise the service, for the time being, the Telecom Regulatory Authority of India (TRAI) has shut down Free Basics. Reliance though continues to offer the service across its network.

What Monsanto has done by pushing Intellectual Property (IP) laws and patents on seeds, Zuckerberg is attempting to do with Internet freedom in India. And like Monsanto, he is targeting the most marginalised Indians. Free Basics sets limits on Internet usage and right at the outset, it had barred streaming video content stating that it would interfere with the telecom companies' services. This despite TRAI's recommendation for making video content more accessible to different populations.

If the service gets the green signal once again what is to stop telecom companies from redefining the Internet to suit their own interests, and those of their corporate partners. After all, the ban on Free Basics has not stopped Reliance from continuing to provide the service to its huge user base, largely farmers.

Why should Zuckerberg decide what a farmer in Punjab should access on the Internet? Should the Internet enable a farmer to understand how the GMO technology has failed everywhere in the world and has only been kept going through unfair market and trade policies? Or should the Internet suggest the next patented molecule he should spray on his crop?

The Monsanto-Facebook connection also runs deep. Nearly all the top-12 investors in the seed company are among the top investors in Facebook. This includes the Vanguard Group, which is a major investor in Deere & Co., Monsanto's partner for 'smart tractors'. It's no surprise, then, that an event page of the March Against Monsanto, a major American grassroots movement in support of labelling and regulating GMOs, was removed by Facebook. The page promoted a rally in Monsanto's headquarters, St. Louis, in August 2013.

The Right to Food is the right to choose what we want to eat; to know what is in our food and to opt for nourishing, tasty food—not the few packaged goods that corporations want us to consume. The Right to the Internet is the right to choose what media and information we want to access; to choose the ecological, political, economic, social and intellectual spaces that enrich us—not what companies think should be our 'basics'. Our right to know what we are eating is as essential as our right to information, all information.

In the ultimate Orwellian doublespeak, 'free' for Zuckerberg means 'privatised', a far cry from privacy, a word the tech entrepreneur does not believe in. And like the corporate-created 'free' trade agreements, Free Basics is anything but free for citizens. Real knowledge comes from experience, interconnectedness, participation. Big Data is not knowledge. Big Data from One Corporation contributes—as The Knowledge Manifesto of the International Commission on the Future of Food states—to 'information obesity'. It is a means of control.

Likewise, forty-two African universities, working with diverse cultures and in diverse ecosystems—deserts and rainforests, mountains and coasts—adopting One Agriculture, One Science programmes is a recipe for impoverishing and enslaving Africa, intellectually and economically.

There are three major reasons why this One Agriculture, One Science initiative (*http://www.oneagonescience.org*) will aggravate problems in agriculture instead of solving them. The branding exercise that resulted in One Agriculture, One Science is a failure in itself. For 'experts' to believe that different climates, different ecosystems and different cultures can be prescribed 'One' solution is absurd. Either they are not aware that the rainfall in Cherrapunji, in northeast India, is not the same as rainfall in Oaxaca, Mexico, or that it's hotter in Maharashtra than in Oregon, or they simply don't care whether a farmer's crop fails or succeeds, as long as they have extracted every last dollar, rupee or rand from our producers.

The One Agriculture push by Big Agricorporations ignores the findings of all UN agencies, including the International Assessment of Agriculture, Knowledge, Science and Technology for Development (IAASTD), a global project which had a team of 400 scientists working to assess the role of agricultural science and technology in reducing hunger and poverty and facilitating socially and economically sustainable development. Their report states, 'We must look to small holder traditional farming to deliver food security in third world countries through agroecological systems which are sustainable. Governments must invest in these systems. This is the clear evidence.'

A collective corporate assault is underway, across the globe. The veterans of corporate America, like Gates, are being joined by the next generation of philanthro-corporate imperialists like Zuckerberg. The similarities between Gates and Zuckerberg's perfectly-rehearsed, PR-managed announcements of 'giving away' their fortunes are uncanny. Whatever entity the Zuckerbergs form to handle the $45 billion they have pledged towards 'the cause of human advancement' will most likely end up being a lot like the Bill and Melinda Gates Foundation—powerful enough to influence climate negotiations during the 2017 One Planet Summit, but responsible for nothing.

What could Gates and Zuckerberg have to gain from dictating terms to governments during the climate summit held in Paris to commemorate the two years of the Paris Climate Accord? 'The Breakthrough Energy Coalition will invest in ideas that have the potential to transform the way we all produce and consume energy', Zuckerberg wrote on his Facebook page, announcing Gates' Breakthrough Energy Coalition, which pools in the combined wealth of hundreds of billions of dollars of 28 private investors who will influence how the world produces and consumes energy.

At the same time, Gates is currently behind a move to force chemical, fossil fuel dependent agriculture and patented GMOs through the Alliance for a Green Revolution in Africa (AGRA) which was founded through a partnership between the Rockefeller Foundation and the Gates Foundation. It is an attempt to trap African farmers into developing a dependence on fossil fuels that should be left underground, as well as on Monsanto for seeds and petrochemicals. The 2017 World Food Prize was given to Dr. Akinwumi Adesina for his critical role in the establishment of AGRA, as Minister of Agriculture in Nigeria. The ceremony was held at the U.S. Department of Agriculture on June 27, 2017. Just as the Green Revolution was imposed on India jointly by the US government and the Rockefeller Foundation, the 'Green Revolution' for Africa is being imposed by Gates, the Rockefeller Foundation and the

The Technology Machine of the 1%

US government. In the world of the 1%, governments are just their extension, their salesmen.

In the five decades since the Green Revolution in India, ecological science has taught us the value of diversity in ensuring sustainability, increasing food production, and resilience. Indian farmers have evolved 2,000,000 varieties of rice; they have evolved thousands of varieties of wheat, pulses and oilseeds; they have evolved thousands of varieties of brinjal, banana and mango. However, One Agriculture, based on One Flawed Science, has no place for their diverse knowledge. It is driven by 'experts' who neither have an understanding of diversity nor a respect for the knowledge of farmers—the very foundation of the science of agroecology.

The manipulation of productivity and output data to suit the false narrative of 'feeding the world with chemicals and GMOs' has led to violence against the planet, with 75 per cent water systems destroyed, 75 per cent soil desertified and degraded, 93 per cent plant biodiversity lost, biodiversity of pollinators threatened, and 40 per cent contributions to climate change. And this industrial system only provides 30 per cent of the food we eat. If the proportion of industrial agriculture in our food system were to increase, we would soon have a dead planet. And no food.

They say that we do not know anything,
That we are backwardness,
That our head needs changing for a better one.
They say that some learned men are saying this about us,
These academics who reproduce themselves,
In our own lives.
What is there on the banks of these rivers, Doctor?
Take out your binoculars

And your spectacles.
Look if you can,
Five hundred flowers,
From five hundred different types of potato
Grow on the terraces
Above abysses
That your eyes don't reach.
Those five hundred flowers
Are my brain,
My flesh.

— Jose Maria Arguedas,
Quechua poet from the Andes

Golden Rice: a blind approach to preventing blindness is not science

Golden Rice is genetically engineered rice with two genes from the daffodil plant and one gene from a bacterium, resulting in a yellow colour that is supposed to increase beta-carotene, a precursor of vitamin A. It is being offered as a miracle cure for Vitamin A Deficiency (VAD).

However, Golden Rice, even if successful, will be 400% less efficient in providing vitamin A than the biodiversity alternatives that women have to offer. To get your daily requirement of vitamin A, all you need to eat is one of the following:

- Two tablespoons of spinach or cholai (amaranth) or radish leaves
- Four tablespoons of mustard or bathua leaves
- One tablespoon of coriander chutney
- One-and-a-half tablespoon of mint chutney

- One carrot
- One mango

Not only do these alternatives provide more vitamin A than Golden Rice ever will, at a lower cost, they also provide other nutrients.

To defend the mirage of Golden Rice, and through it the failed GMO technologies, in 2016, 107 Nobel Laureates were mobilised (including the ghosts of dead ones–Alfred G. Gilman died on December 23, 2015) to validate its claims. It was a clumsy and crude PR stunt and had nothing to do with 'science'.

The Nobel letter, issued on June 29, 2016, tries to promote Golden Rice urging 'Greenpeace and its supporters to re-examine the experience of farmers and consumers worldwide with crops and foods improved through biotechnology, recognize the findings of authoritative scientific bodies and regulatory agencies, and abandon their campaign against "GMOs" in general and Golden Rice in particular'.

The letter coincided with the vote on the DARK Act in the US Senate. Christened the 'Deny Americans the Right-to-Know' Act by the critics, the Act that prevents United States from labelling GMOs was moved through Congress by Republican Congressman Mike Pompeo, who initially was the CIA Director in the Trump administration and is now the Secretary of State.

What could be more unscientific and fraudulent than using the signatures of dead scientists. This is Fraud Number 1. Trying to substitute expertise with the 'authority' of Nobel Prize winners is Fraud Number 2. Philip Stark, Associate Dean, Division of Mathematical and Physical Sciences and Professor of Statistics at the University of California, Berkeley, presented his own analysis of the expertise of the signatories on Twitter: '1 peace prize,

8 economists, 24 physicists, 33 chemists, 41 doctors'. He added that science is 'about evidence not authority. What do they know of agriculture? Done relevant research? Science is supposed to be "show me", not "trust me"... Nobel Prize or not.'

Fraud Number 3 is that it was Monsanto and Co's PR men, including Jay Byrne, who actually orchestrated the Nobel Laureate mobilisation. Byrne is the former head of corporate communications for Monsanto. Trying to pass off a PR stunt as scientific debate and discourse is a scientific fraud.

Fraud Number 4 is substituting reason and evidence with an ad hominem attack, which has no place in real science.

Fraud Number 5 is presenting a failed scientific experiment as a miracle, and blaming Greenpeace for the failure of the GMO technology. As Glenn Stone, a rice scientist at Washington University in St Louis, Missouri, has stated, 'The simple fact is that after 24 years of research and breeding, Golden Rice is still years away from being ready for release.'[47]

According to Stone, 'The rice simply has not been successful in test plots of the rice-breeding institutes in the Philippines, where the leading research is being done. It has not even been submitted for approval to the regulatory agency, the Philippine Bureau of Plant Industry (BPI).' In 2015, the Supreme Court of the Philippines had issued a temporary suspension of GMO crop trials at the International Rice Research Institute(IRRI).

Dr Allison Wilson, in her paper, 'Goodbye to Golden Rice? GM Trait Leads to Drastic Yield Loss and "Metabolic Meltdown"', points out,

> Golden Rice has never been commercialised, however, and its failure to reach the market has been blamed on 'over-regulation' and on 'anti-GMO' opposition. Recent research by Indian scientists shows that introducing Golden Rice transgenes had unexpected

detrimental effects. Their high yielding and agronomically superior Indian rice variety became pale and stunted, with yields so reduced it was unsuitable for cultivation (Bollinedi,et al. 2017).This research has obvious implications for Golden Rice, particularly by suggesting that nutritionally useful GMO Golden Rice may be an impossibility.[48]

All plants inherantly have diverse nutrients. Industrial agriculture produces nutritionally empty commodities not only because the soil is deprived of nutrition by not restoring the diverse nutrients through organic matter, but also because monocultures decrease the diversity of nutrients that are provided by biodiversity. 'Biofortification' is genetic engineering through which the nutritional value of crops is 'increased', like the Golden Rice that is 'fortified' with vitamin A or banana 'fortified' with iron.

Gates is propping up failed Golden Rice, rejected GMO brinjal, and useless GMO banana. He funded one scientist in Australia to biofortify bananas with iron, in the name of saving women who died of iron deficiency during child-birth. Women in India started a campaign to say 'No to GMO banana', showing that it would be 7,000% less effective as a source of iron than the bananas we have. The GMO banana project for iron fortification in India went underground and was resurrected as a vitamin A deficiency project in Uganda.

It is now more than twenty years since the miracle of so-called Golden Rice has been promoted as a cure for vitamin A deficiency.[49] The last time the Golden Rice myth was resurrected was when Patrick Moore of Golden Rice Now! was sent to Asia to promote the failed promise. Women across the world, organised as Diverse Women for Diversity, issued a declaration on International Women's Day 2015 that 'Women and biodiversity feed the world, not corporations and GMOs.'[50]

Bill Gates specially set up the Cornell Alliance for Science to promote failed biotechnology by erasing the scientific evidence on the ground, of the failure of GMOs, and substituting it with propaganda pieces to attack local farmers, journalists and scientists as 'anti-science'.

To prevent real science and the reality of GMO failures from reaching the world, he finances a PR institute that masquerades as a scientific institution. Originally endowed with $5.6 million by the Gates Foundation in August 2014, the Cornell Alliance for Science received 'a renewed contribution' of $6.4 million in 2017. The new grant takes the total Gates contribution to $12 million.[51]

Cornell uses Mark Lynas, a one-time vociferous opposer of GMOs, to fly into different countries to falsify the GMO story. Journalist and author Lynas is new at the Cornell Alliance for Science and is sent to the deficient parts of the world to marginalise people's voices and put out the biotech industry propaganda. When Bt brinjal failed in Bangladesh, he was sent to drown the local news of its failure through a planted story in *The New York Times*. When peasants disrupted the GMO Golden Rice trials in the Phillipines, he was sent to muzzle the the farmers' perspective and voices on GMOs.

Gates and his expanding patent empire

Biopiracy of climate resilience in farmers' varieties

While talking 'innovation' Gates has engaged in piracy, from software to seeds. At the Expo Milano 2015, during the Women's Forum organised by Emma Bonino (Italy's former foreign minister), I was invited to make the keynote address. In a panel following my address, a representative of the Gates Foundation talked of how it was financing the innovation and invention of climate resilient crops through new technologies. When I asked him which farmers' varieties they were using, he was silent.

Climate resilience is a complex trait and cannot be 'engineered' through the crude tools of transferring single gene traits from one organism to another. What corporations and the Gates Foundation are doing is taking farmers' varieties with known climate resilient traits from public gene banks, mapping their genome, and taking out patents on the basis of guesswork and speculation about which part of the genome contributes to the known trait.

Along coastal areas in India, farmers have evolved flood tolerant and salt tolerant varieties of rice, such as Bhundi, Kalambank, Lunabakada, Sankarchin, Nalidhulia, Ravana, Seulapuni, and Dhosarakhuda. Crops, such as millets, have been evolved for drought tolerance to provide food security in water-scarce regions, and during water-scarce years.

Navdanya decided to save the vanishing rice diversities of Odisha through a system of germ-plasm-conservation, employing both in situ and ex situ methods and, at the same time, carrying out experiments on their sustainability in varied eco-climatic conditions, in view of rapid climate change and yield potentials under various soil amendments. Their behaviours and responses are being recorded. This has come in handy while selecting the seeds of specific rice diversities for empowering local communities to rehabilitate agriculture in disaster areas like Erasama in Odisha after the super cyclone of 1999, Nagapattinam in Tamil Nadu after the Boxing Day tsunami in 2005, and Nandigram in Bengal in 2007.

The tsunami waves affected agriculture due to the intrusion of seawater and deposit of sea land. More than 5,203.73 hectares of agricultural land in Nagapattinam were affected. The Navdanya team conducted a study in the impacted villages to facilitate agricultural recovery. We distributed three saline resistant varieties of paddy, which included Bhundi, Kalambank and Lunabakada, to farmers in the worst-affected areas. A total of 100 quintals were collected from Navdanya farmers in Odisha and transported over a distance of more than 1,500 kilometres from Balasore to Nagapattinam under the 'seeds of hope' programme; the yield from these varieties was three times greater and far better than any other known high yielders. The same varieties behaved even better when cultivated in Indonesia, another 1,000 or more kilometres away, in 2006, by Professor Friedhelm Golten of Hohenheim University in Germany.

Patenting life through genetic engineering is rapidly giving way to patenting life through mapping the genome. Navdanya's Community Seed Bank in Odisha has conserved more than 800 rice varieties and multiplied and distributed salt-tolerant and flood-tolerant varieties, wherever required.

The 'innovation' necessary for the evolution of these climate-resilient traits has occurred cumulatively and collectively over thousands of years. These traits and crops are a commons. However, they are being presented as the 'inventions' of 'scientists', who rename the flood-tolerant property in the farmer's variety (such as Dhullaputia from Odisha) as Sub1A or the submergence-tolerant gene. Using marker-assisted selection (not transgenics) researchers were able to isolate the submergence-tolerant gene, Sub1A, and then transfer it to a rice variety, known as Swarna, that is grown on more than five million hectares in India and Bangladesh. Most rice varieties can tolerate flooding for only a few days, but researchers say that Swarna-Sub1 can withstand submergence for two weeks without affecting yields.

This is a scientifically flawed claim, based on genetic reductionism, because flood tolerance, like other climate-resilient traits such as salt tolerance and drought tolerance, are multi-genetic traits; they cannot be identified as *a* Sub1A gene. Because it is not 'a gene', it has been referred to as Submergence Tolerance 1 (Sub1) Quantitative Trait Locus (QTL).

What marker-assisted selection does is to identify the genetic sequence that is always linked to varieties which share a trait.[52] Such varieties are then selected for crossing conventionally with varieties like Swarna. Farmers who bred the traits did not need market oriented selection to breed for climate resilience. This is why we need to recognise the diversity and pluralism of knowledge systems as well as the diversity of languages to describe and name processes and organisms.

The agrochemical and biotech industry is using the climate resilient crops bred by farmers for their genome mapping, claiming the farmer-bred traits as inventions through patents. But this is not breeding, it is piracy, biopiracy. And this is how the Gates Foundation redefines the biopiracy of flood-tolerant rice from Indian farmers—an 'innovation' funded by Gates.

Corporations have taken out more than 1,500 climate resilient patents on crops. In 2014, India's patent office rejected Monsanto's application for climate-resilient traits of cold tolerance, salt tolerance and drought tolerance in crop varieties evolved by farmers over millennia, through applying their knowledge of breeding. While the spin is that these traits are being genetically engineered, the reality is that its biopiracy. Unlike farmers who knew what they were doing when they selected and bred for specific traits, corporations have no idea. Their genome mapping is done through computer programmes and guesswork about which part of the genome contributes to which trait. The 'privatisers' of today include not just the corporations which are becoming fewer and larger through mergers, but also individuals like Bill Gates.

Digital piracy of life: 'mining' genetic data with DivSeek

Diversity Seek (DivSeek) is a global project launched in 2015 to map the genetic data of the peasant diversity of seeds held in gene banks. It is an extractive project to 'mine' the data in the seed and to 'censor' out the commons.[53]

The partnering organisations of DivSeek include the Consultative Group for International Agricultural Research (CGIAR) centres, and public universities like Cornell and Iowa State which are being increasingly privatised by the biotechnology industry and by Bill Gates. There are seven million crop accessions in public seed banks. DivSeek could enable only five corporations to own this diversity. Cornell is where the Gates Foundation funds the propaganda machine through the Cornell Alliance for Science. Iowa State University is where Gates funds the unethical human feeding trials of GMO bananas. The Foundation also funds the partners of DivSeek, especially the African Agricultural Technology Foundation, and an Africa-Brazil collaboration in DivSeek.[54] This genetic colonialism is nothing but an enclosure of the genetic commons. A number of mass sequencing projects, such as G2P-SOL, which plans to deep sequence 50,000 *solanaceae* (nightshade) seeds; Bean-Adapt; and The 3,000 Chickpea Genome Initiative, are under way. The plants primarily originate in developing countries, especially Latin America and Asia.

The Technology Machine of the 1%

Farmers' rights to the seeds they have evolved over millennia will be open to biopiracy through the genome databases, just as maps were used to claim and steal territory in an earlier colonialism. And just as prior claims of communities were erased, all local laws ignored and violated, DivSeek is trying to bypass all access and benefit sharing provisions consistent with the Convention on Biological Diversity and, for some plants, the International Treaty on Plant Genetic Resources for Food and Agriculture (ITPGRFA). Key DivSeek members are inclined to ignore a resolution of the ITPGRFA, adopted during the Sixth Session of the Governing Body of the ITPGRFA in October 2015, asking them to report on the policy implications of DivSeek technologies.

Ignoring the rights of farmers and treaties that protect biodiversity and create obligation for access, DivSeek is considering a Syngenta-inspired scheme to sell access to the sequence data of farmers' seeds from international gene banks.

Evogene Ltd. (Israel) has patented a computer programme for reading the plant genome; its proprietary in silico 'gene discovery technology' is called ATHLETE™ (in silico, as opposed to in vivo or in vitro, refers to investigations performed through the use of a computer or computer simulation). ATHLETE is a computer database and analysis programme for finding gene function by comparing sequences from as many different plant species, tissues, organs, and growth conditions as possible. Evogene claims its database has eight million expressed sequences, 4,00,000 'proprietary gene clusters', and 30 plant species. The programme clusters sequences according to a variety of criteria, and then determines which gene candidates to investigate further. It is an informed winnowing process.

ETC Group's report 'Capturing "Climate Genes"' explains how:

ATHLETE uses vast amounts of available genomic data (mostly public) to rapidly reach a reliable limited list of candidate key genes with high relevance to a target trait of choice. Allegorically, the ATHLETE platform could be viewed as a 'machine' that is able to choose 50-100 lottery tickets from amongst hundreds of thousands of tickets, with the high likelihood that the winning ticket will be included among them.

Evogene also collaborates with Monsanto. A deal struck between the two companies gives Monsanto exclusive rights to a number of genes identified by Evogene that reportedly allow crops to maintain stable yields with lower applications of nitrogen. The companies collaborate on drought tolerance traits as well. Monsanto and BASF (the world's third ranking agrochemical company) are investing $1.5 billion on collaborative R&D to develop high-yielding crops that are more tolerant to adverse environmental conditions such as drought.

Like ATHLETE, DivSeek is based on the digital mapping of farmers' seeds. As Marie Haga of Global Crop Diversity Trust says,

> Agricultural biodiversity is more important than ever, it is the prerequisite for food security...By combining the information we have on where plants grow, information about their physical characteristics and the sequencing data or the plants' DNA, we should be able to speed up the breeding processes.

Whereas Cornell University's maize geneticist, Edward Buckler contends that 'the big issue of our times is the "dematerialisation" of germplasm. Germplasm is becoming the information technology that it always was.'

Biopiracy is being addressed by laws that have been framed at international and national levels. It generally refers to the illegal appropriation of biological diversity and the traditional knowledge of local communities from developing countries by multinational corporations and research institutions. This definition mainly covers two aspects: (1) access and use of biological material or traditional knowledge without the authorisation of the country of origin and the indigenous communities that hold and develop these resources; and/or (2) lack of benefit sharing, or unjust and unfair sharing of benefits with the countries and communities who provided the resources. These forms of biopiracy are expressly prohibited by Articles 15 and 8(j) of the Convention on Biological Diversity (CBD), 1992, and, more recently, the Nagoya Protocol on access and benefit sharing, adopted by the Conference of the Parties to the CBD at its tenth meeting on October 29, 2010. At the national level, many developing countries have adopted legislation regulating access to their genetic resources and requiring benefit sharing in accordance with the principles of the CBD, such as, the Biological Diversity Act, 2002, in India. The country is, in fact, one of the ten megadiverse countries in the world, accounting for 7.8 per cent of the global recorded species.

At a DivSeek seminar, held from November 28 to December 1, 2016, at the Rockefeller Foundation's Bellagio Center in Italy, 18 experts discussed 'game-changing and potentially disruptive DNA-sequencing technologies, big-data platforms, high performance computing, image-based phenotyping methods, gene-editing techniques, and synthetic biology concepts', concepts, reveals the TWN Briefing Paper-2016.

The case of the CRISPR

CRISPR has been described as 'a relatively easy way to alter any organism's DNA, just as a computer user can edit a word in a document'. A 2015 article in *Forbes* magazine explains, 'Four years ago, the protein called CRISPR-Cas9, an enzyme that bacteria use to attack viruses that infect them, was unknown to humans. Now it is ubiquitous in science labs as the most efficient way yet invented of cutting-and-pasting DNA. *Wired* magazine, in a breathless cover story, just called it "The Genesis Engine", instructing readers to "buckle up" because the "easy DNA editing CRISPR...will change the world"'.[55]

However, a new study published in *Nature Methods* revealed that CRISPR introduced hundreds of unintended mutations into the genome of mice.[56] It found more than 1,500 single-nucleotide mutations and more than 100 larger deletions and insertions. None of these DNA mutations were predicted by the computer algorithms that are widely used by researchers to screen the genome of an organism to look for potential off-target effects.

As of now, it is technically not possible to make a single (and only a single) genetic change to a genome using CRISPR and to ensure that it has done so.[57] As Franziska Fichtner notes, 'in mammalian systems Cas9 causes a high degree of off-target effects'. And Jonathan Latham cautions, ordinary CRISPR 'can induce mutations at sites that differ by as many as five nucleotides from the intended target'; in other words, CRISPR may act at unknown sites in the genome where it is not wanted.[58]

The third error that CRISPR makes is to imply that changes to gene functions can be presumed to be discrete and constrained. The concept of the precise editing of a genome, leading to a precise biological outcome, depends heavily on the conception that genes give rise to simple outputs. This is the genetic paradigm taught in school. It is also the paradigm presented to the public, one that even plays a large role in the thinking of molecular genetic researchers.

However, a defined, discrete or simple pathway from gene to trait probably does not exist. Most gene function is mediated murkily through highly complex biochemical and other networks that depend on many conditional factors, such as the presence of other genes and their variants, on the environment, on the age of the organism, on chance, and so forth. Geneticists and molecular biologists, however, ever since the time of Gregor Mendel, have striven to find or create artificial experimental systems in which environmental and any other sources of variation are minimised so as not to distract from the more 'important' business of genetic discovery.

But by discarding organisms or traits that do not follow their expectations, geneticists and molecular biologists have constructed a circular argument in favour of a naive deterministic account of gene function. Their paradigm habitually downplays the enormous complexities by which information passes (in both directions) between organisms and their genomes. It has created an immense and mostly unexamined bias in the default public understanding of genes and DNA. This indicates just how unreliable the assumptions and projections of genome editing techniques like CRISPR are; and how unreliable the claims that they are precise, predictable, and therefore safe, and not in need of biosafety regulation.

Bill Gates and 13 others have invested $120 million in a CRISPR-based new company, EDITAS, founded by Feng Zhang of the Massachusetts Institute of Technology (MIT) and the Broad Institute. The other investors are Deerfield Management, Viking Global Investors, Fidelity Management &

Research Company, funds and accounts managed by T. Rowe Price Associates, Inc., Google Ventures, Jennison Associates on behalf of certain clients, Khosla Ventures, EcoR1 Capital, Casdin Capital, Omega Funds, Cowen Private Investments and Alexandria Venture Investments. The lead investor is a newly created firm called bng0, a select group led by Boris Nikolic, who was previously a science advisor to Bill Gates. Both EDITAS and Gates'office confirm that the Microsoft billionaire is among the bng0 backers.[59]

Gates also funds Jennifer Doudna, who co-founded Caribou Biosciences to work on the research uses of CRISPR-Cas9, and, more recently, set up Intellia Therapeutics to work on disease treatments. Doudna and EDITAS are engaged in a patent battle on CRISPR technologies. With Gates funding both sides involved in the patent battle, no matter who loses, Gates wins, as he is directly investing in corporations taking out patents on CRISPR.

The patent application for CRISPR by the University of Harvard includes a long list of over 50 weeds and almost 200 herbicides that the technology could be used against, thereby laying out a business case for licensing the patent to major agrochemical companies.

EDITAS Medicine—which has licensed one of the patents in question—disclosed that till 2016 it has spent $10.9 million on legal fees incurred by the Broad Institute and Harvard, mostly to defend patents awarded for CRISPR inventions by Feng Zhang. That cost is over and above the $4.7 million spent in 2015. In a statement, the company said, 'Investing in intellectual property is one component how we are building the company to be a leader in genome medicine,' adding that it reimburses Broad and Harvard for expenses 'associated with the prosecution and maintenance of the patent rights that we license from them.'[60]

Further, Bayer, a $96 billion German drug company, will provide the Basel-based CRISPR Therapeutics a minimum of $300 million over the next five years, from 2016, to develop the CRISPR-Cas9 gene editing technology to treat conditions such as blood disorders, blindness, and congenital heart disease. Bayer is also acquiring a majority stake in CRISPR Therapeutics for $35 million.[61]

Bayer CropScience joins Astra Zeneca and Nestlé Health Science as strategic innovation partners in Flagship Ventures Fund V that will focus on innovations in healthcare and sustainability in the energy, water, agriculture and nutrition sectors.[62]

The ethical issues surrounding CRISPR are significant. A *New York Times* report says, 'Scientists are worried that it could also be used to alter genes in human embryos, sperm or eggs in ways that can be passed from generation to generation. The prospect raises fears of a dystopian future in which scientists create an elite population of designer babies with enhanced intelligence, beauty or other traits.'[63]

Sequences are frequently repeated within a genome, often as an artefact of evolution, and scientists have expressed the concern that there is mounting evidence that gene editing can have unpredictable 'off-target effects', i.e., it may cut and replace not only the target gene but other genes with the same partial sequence elsewhere in the genome. Finally, Ricardo Steinbrecher notes that in some countries CRISPR is falling into a regulatory void; the US Department of Agriculture (USDA) declined to regulate a CRISPR-engineered mushroom in 2016, saying it was outside USDA's biotech regulations. CRISPR has become the window for the biotech industry to continue the failed GMO experiment. Monsanto has signed an agreement for agriculture applications of CRISPR with the Broad Institute.[64]

Bill Gates, biodiversity, gene drives, and new GMOs: from the terminator to the exterminator

DARPA (Pentagon's research arm) and the Bill and Melinda Gates Foundation sponsored a 2016 report by the National Academy of Sciences (NAS) in the United States, titled 'Gene Drives on the Horizon: Advancing Science, Navigating Uncertainty, and Aligning Research with Public Values', which warns: 'One possible goal of release of a gene-drive modified organism is to cause the extinction of the target species or a drastic reduction in its abundance.'

Gene drives have been called 'mutagenic chain reactions', and are to the biological world what chain reactions are to the nuclear world. *The Guardian* describes gene drives as the 'gene bomb'. Kevin Esvelt of the MIT exclaims, 'a release anywhere is likely to be a release everywhere', and asks, 'do you really have the right to run an experiment where if you screw up, it affects the whole world?'

The NAS report cites the case of wiping out amaranth as an example of 'potential benefit'. Yet, the 'magical technology' of gene drives remains a ghost, or the US government's Department of Defence's secret 'weapon' to continue its war on *amaranthus culturis*. Seventy-five years ago, DARPA-Mind began its extermination experiment, and sent humanity off-axis. (DARPA is Pentagon's research agency and DARPA-Mind is our label for the militarised mind.) The chemicals, materials, and technologies acquired during the war, and patented, were forced on *amaranthus culturis*.

The following objective and rationale have been stated in the NAS report,

Case Study 6: Controlling Palmer Amaranth To Increase Agriculture Productivity

Objective
Create gene drives in Palmer amaranth (*Amaranthus palmeri* also called pigweed) to reduce or eliminate the weed on agricultural fields in the Southern United States.

Rationale
Palmer amaranth infests agricultural fields throughout the American South. It has evolved resistance to the herbicide glyphosate, the world's most-used herbicide, and this resistance has become geographically widespread.

Palmer amaranth has emerged as one of the world's superweeds. Instead of seeing its emergence as a superweed as a result of the failure of misguided herbicide resistant GMOs, Monsanto & Co. (investors, scientists, corporations, DARPA, and Gates) are now rushing to drive the amaranth species to extinction through the deployment of an untested tool. The NAS report casually states the 'potential human harms of gene drives':

Gene drives developed for agricultural purposes could also have adverse effects on human well-being. Transfer of a suppression drive to a non-target wild species could have both adverse environmental outcomes and harmful effects on vegetable crops, for example. Palmer amaranth in Case Study 6 is a damaging weed in the United States, but related *amaranthus* species are cultivated for food in Mexico, South America, India, and China.

From the high slopes of the Himalaya, through the plains of north, central and south India, to the coastlines of the east, west

107

and south, amaranth is a web of life. In fact, the Himalayan region is one of the 'centres of diversity' for the amarnath. Its leaves contain more iron than spinach, and have a much more delicate flavour. Apart from rice bran, the grain of the amaranth has the highest content of iron among cereals. One kilogram of amaranth flour, added to one kilogram of refined wheat flour, increases its iron content from 25 miligrams to 245 miligrams. Adding amaranth flour to wheat/rice flour is a cheaper and healthier way to prevent nutritional anaemia rather than buying expensive tablets, tonics, health drinks, branded and bio fortified flour, or canned spinach.

The amaranth is extremely rich in complex carbohydrates and proteins, too. It has 12-18 per cent more protein than other cereals, particularly lysine, a critical amino acid. It also differs from other cereals in that 65 per cent of it is found in the germ and 35 per cent in the endosperm, compared to an average of 15 per cent in the germ and 85 per cent in the endosperm in other cereals. The amaranth grain is about the richest source of calcium, other than milk; it has 390 gms of calcium compared to 10 gms in rice and 23 gms in refined flour.

Industrial agriculture treated amaranth greens as 'weed', and tried to exterminate it with herbicides. Then came Monsanto, with Roundup Ready crops, genetically engineered to resist the spraying of Roundup so that the GMO crop would survive the otherwise lethal chemical, while everything else that was green perished.

Financialisation, patentisation and forced digitisation

In the twenty-first century, the corporate empire has found new instruments of extraction, with patents and (what should be called) 'capitalisation', being the two most prominent ones. While the chemical/biotech/seed industry 'innovated' and 'invented' patents on life and on seeds, as a means to extract profits from farmers, the second instrument, financialisation of the economy, is equally perverse. It has marginalised the real wealth that people produce in real economies, and rewarded primarily the capitalists. The financial economy is now 70 times bigger than the real economy in the world. The concentration of the world's wealth in the hands of the 1% is a consequence of patentisation, financialisation, and the digitisation of our lives. The most recent bait and switch that has been used by globalised corporate power to worm its way into households in India is the sudden demonetisation of large denomination notes. Towards the end of 2016 there was a concerted and coercive attempt to impose a digital economy on the country through a 'cash ban'. Those without smartphones and credit cards were overnight converted into 'digital barbarians', needing to be 'civilised' and mainstreamed through 'digital literacy'.

The 'demonetisation' of India's economy at the stroke of midnight on November 8, 2016, was a gamble by corporates to appropriate people's wealth by locking it behind an encryption key, shutting down people's economies overnight by allowing only those sections of the economy willing to indulge the payment gateway-keeper to operate. Naspers Group is that gatekeeper for Digital India.

More than 90 per cent of India functions on cash to sustain the people's economy. By withdrawing 86 per cent of all currency overnight and declaring it illegal, the damage inflicted on the majority of ordinary Indians was collosal.

Just as patents on seeds were an illegitimate attempt at criminalising farmers by making seed saving illegal, 'demonetisation' was an illegitimate attempt at criminalising people's savings and seriously disturbing their economy, which comprises 80 per cent of India's real economy.

Bill Gates, in his speech for the *NITI-Lecture Series: Transforming India*, delivered in the presence of Prime Minister Narendra Modi and his Cabinet colleagues, stated: 'the government's bold move to demonetise high-value denominations and replace them with new notes with high security features was an important step to move away from the shadow economy to a more transparent economy.' He further said that digital transactions would rise dramatically as a result, and, in the next several years, make India one of the most digitised economies not just by size, but by percentage as well.[65]

The Oxfam report on the economy of the 1% states that 188 of the 201 leading companies in the world have a presence in at least one tax haven.[66] Nine out of ten World Economic Forum (WEF) corporate partners have a presence in at least one tax haven and it is estimated that tax dodges by multinational corporations cost developing countries at least $100 billion every year. A global network of tax havens further enables the richest individuals to hide $7.6 trillion. If taxes were paid on the income that this wealth generates, an extra $190 billion would be available to governments every year.

The report, 'Gated Development–Is the Gates Foundation Always a Force for Good?', by Global Justice Now, argues that what the Bill and Melinda Gates Foundation (BMGF) is doing could end up exacerbating global inequality by entrenching corporate power, globally. It raises a serious concern regarding tax dodging by the Foundation and its close links with corporate interests.

A 2012 report by the US Senate found that Microsoft's

use of offshore subsidiaries enabled it to avoid taxes of up to $4.5 billion, a sum greater than the BMGF's annual grant making ($3.6 billion in 2014).

'How Piracy Opens Doors for Windows', a *Los Angeles Times* article,[67] quotes Bill Gates,

> Although about 3 million computers get sold every year in China, people don't pay for the software. Someday they will, though.... And as long as they're going to steal it, we want them to steal ours. They'll get sort of addicted, and then we'll somehow figure out how to collect sometime in the next decade.

Gates' payment portals are here to collect.

The war on cash is a war unleashed by those who will earn huge profits by making cash illegal. These include the Better Than Cash Alliance, Gates Foundation (Microsoft), Omidyar Network (eBay), Dell Foundation, Mastercard, Visa, and Metlife Foundation. Like the Green Revolution, the Digital Revolution was conceived in the US, and launched by a partnership between global business, robber barons and the US government. The Green Revolution, based on oil, was pushed by the Rockefeller Foundation; the Digital Revolution, based on 'bytes', has been pushed by Bill Gates. Neither was a sovereign choice made by India.

While both chemical farming then and digital payments now were and are presented as the next step in technological progress chosen by the people, both are in fact, a result of coercion and intense lobbying.

In terms of financial costs, and ecological and social costs, no one opts for costlier tools. Socially and ecologically destructive tools are not chosen, they have to be imposed.

On October 14, 2016, just four weeks before demonetisation

Top 30 Companies with the Most Money Held Offshore

Company	Amount Held Offshore ($millions)	Number of Tax Haven Subsidiaries	Company	Amount Held Offshore ($millions)	Number of Tax Haven Subsidiaries
Apple	241,900	3	PepsiCo	40,200	135
Pfizer	193,587	181	J.P. Morgan Chase & Co.	34,600	385
Microsoft	124,000	5	Amgen	32,600	9
General Electric	104,000	20	Coca-Cola	31,900	15
International Business Machines	68,100	16	United Technologies	29,000	31
Merck	59,200	125	Qualcomm	28,800	3
Google	58,300	1	Goldman Sachs Group	28,550	987
Cisco Systems	58,000	56	Gilead Sciences	28,500	12
Johnson & Johnson	58,000	62	Intel	26,900	13
Exxon Mobil	51,000	35	Eli Lilly	26,500	33
Proctor & Gamble	49,000	35	Walmart	26,100	–
Hewlett-Packard	47,200	95	AbeVie, Inc.	25,000	38
Chevron	45,400	8	Bristol-Myers Squibb	25,000	23
Citigroup	45,200	140	Danaher	23,500	31
Oracle	42,600	5	Philip Morris International	23,000	7
			Total:	1,648,637	2,509

Source: http://www.oxfamamerica.org/press/top-50-us-companies-stash-16-trillion-offshore/

in India, USAID had announced the establishment of Catalyst: Inclusive Cashless Payment Partnership, in collaboration with India's Ministry of Finance, with the 'goal of effecting a quantum leap in cashless payment in India'. Badal Malick, CEO of Catalyst and former Vice President of Snapdeal, India's most important online marketplace, commented,

> Catalyst's mission is to solve multiple coordination problems that have blocked the penetration of digital payments among merchants and low-income consumers. We look forward to creating a sustainable and replicable model. (…) While there has been (…) a concerted push for digital payments by the government, there is still a last mile gap when it comes to merchant acceptance and coordination issues. We want to bring a holistic ecosystem approach to these problems.

A January 2016 USAID commissioned study titled, 'Beyond Cash', states, 'Merchants, like consumers, are trapped in cash ecosystems, which inhibits their interest in digital payments. Since few traders accept digital payments, few consumers have an interest in it, and since few consumers use it, few traders have an interest in it. Given that banks and payment providers charge a fee for equipment to use or even just try out digital payment, a strong external impulse is needed to achieve a level of card penetration that would create mutual interest of both sides in digital payment options.'

Jonathan Addleton, USAID Mission Director to India said, 'India is at the forefront of global efforts to digitise economies and create new economic opportunities that extend to hard-to-reach populations. Catalyst will support these efforts by focusing on the challenge of making everyday purchases cashless.'[68]

As India floundered in the catastrophic rush to force the country into a digital economy overnight, it became important to pause and reflect on what the digital economy is, who controls the platforms and lines, as well some basic concepts about money and technology which have moulded our lives and our freedoms, based on patented systems. 'Short term pain for long term gain' became the Prime Minister's slogan for the dictated transition to a digital economy. But the pain was not short term, and the gain has been illuisionary, as we know now. In order to assess the long term gain, we need to ask basic questions like: long term gain for whom? By what means? To what end?

Two sets of means, money and technology, come together in what has been declared the real reason for demonetisation—a push towards a digital economy. In the process, means have been elevated to human ends. Why else is every government department directing its energy at making Indians 'digitally literate'?

Imposing the digital economy through a 'cash ban' is a form of technological dictatorship. Economic diversity and technological pluralism are India's strength; it is 'hard cash' that insulated India from the global market's 'dive into the red' in 2008. The currency notes we exchange state, 'I promise to pay the bearer the sum of ...' and the promise is made by the Governor of the Reserve Bank of India. On that promise and trust rests an entire economy, from the local to the national level. At the very least, the demonetisation circus of 2016-17 'busted the trust' in the Indian economy, and inflicted grevious injury on hundreds of thousands of poor people in the informal, non-digitised economy.

In a cash economy, when you exchange Rs 100 even a hundred times it remains Rs 100. In the digital world, those who control the exchange, through digital and financial networks, make money at every step of the 100 exchanges. That is how the digital economy has created the billionaire class of the 1% which controls the economy of the 100%. Real money, reflecting real work, circulates in a circular economy. Digital money is extracted to a global financial system, and it ruptures the law of return on which the circular economy works.

The Technology Machine of the 1%

Gates was preparing for demonetisation before it was undemocratically forced on all Indians in November 2016. Similarly, Gates and Microsoft launched Microsoft Dynamics AX and Microsoft Azure platforms for filing Goods and Services Tax (GST), the new tax system in India, before the government announced it at the stroke of midnight on July 1, 2017.[69]

A few months after forced digitisation through demonetisation, the Indian government took a second step through GST, a digital tax system, described as India's 'biggest tax reform'. A blog on Microsoft Azure explains GST as: 'essentially one new indirect tax system for the whole nation, which will make India one unified common market, right from the manufacturer to the consumer. It is a broad-based, comprehensive, single indirect tax which will be levied concurrently on goods and services across India.'

Although initially businesses were directed to file the return in three stages—submitting the GSTR-1, GSTR-2 and GSTR-3 form every month—according to media reports, after a meeting of the GST Council in May 2018 it was decided to do away with the 'current three-stage return filing process and move to [a] one monthly return [process]'. It was added that the Centre and state governments have agreed to implement the new mechanism in six months 'to ensure adequate preparation for the transition'. Declared as 'among the most complex [GST systems] in the world, with not only one of the highest tax rates but also one of the largest number of tax slabs', by the World Bank's India Development Update report, the roll out of this tax system has been fraught with implementation challenges as well as changes.

Microsoft's Dynamics 365 software collaborates with Easemy GST, a software designed for GST returns by a company in

Gurugram, Haryana, to convert the 'digital barbarians', living, producing and consuming, selling and buying in a self-organised, autopoietic economy into becoming GST compliant and be forced into paying rent to the 1% economy.[70]

Amit Kumar, General Manager, Small and Mid-Market Solutions and Partners at Microsoft India says about GST,

> For every technology major in the country, Small and Medium Enterprises (SMEs) represent the holy grail of opportunity. With around 40 million SMEs in the country, for Microsoft it is no different. For years, through its ambitious 'partner network', Microsoft has been trying to reach out to this audience and it has now received a shot in the arm. The Goods and Services Tax has forced and hastened technology adoption among SMEs.[71]

Bill Gates is considered exceptional because of his Foundation, which, according to *Forbes*, is the richest funder in the world, with assets worth $43.5 billion and disproportionate influence on economic, agriculture and health policies, worldwide. Through his model of philanthrocapitalism, Gates is, in fact, using his unaccountable money power to bypass democratic structures of society, derail the diversity of alternatives available and impose his totalitarian ideas based on One Science, One Agriculture, One History, to shape the future according to his vision. Yet, it is precisely through this so-called philanthropy that Gates is carving out new colonies; *The Financial Times* writes, 'through the stroke of his pen on his cheque book, Gates probably now has the power to affect the lives and well-being of a larger number of his fellow humans than any other private individual in history.' Gates is the Pope, king, queen and merchant adventurer, all-in-one. His decrees are shaping every field—health, education, agriculture, economy, and finance. The fundamentalist faith he is imposing is the worship of the tools he owns through patents.

On a planet with 300 million species and seven billion humans, one man determining the future of the earth and humanity is a dangerous idea. It is dangerous for the earth because the anthropocentric, reductionist, and mechanistic assumptions by which Gates is guided are at the root of the ecological crisis that has brought us to the brink. It dangerous for society because it discounts the contributions of women, indigenous people, and small farmers to knowledge systems and food systems. It is dangerous for the economy because it is blind to the diversity of economies that sustains people's lives, and allows them to take care of the earth and of each other. It defines the economy of the 1% as the only economy, thus implying the economic exclusion of the 99%. It is dangerous for democracy because people should be involved in making the decisions that shape their lives and their futures. One rich man deciding what we will grow and eat, how we will heal ourselves, what we will learn, and what we will think is a dictatorship, not a democracy.

The Global Justice Now report cited earlier argues that what the BMGF is doing could end up exacerbating global inequality and entrenching corporate power. Not only is the Foundation profiting from numerous investments in a series of controversial companies which contribute to economic and social injustice, it is also actively supporting many of those companies, including Monsanto, Dupont and Bayer, through a variety of pro-corporate initiatives around the world.

The BMGF funds projects in which agricultural and pharmaceutical corporations are among the leading beneficiaries, and often invests in the very same companies it is funding; it has an interest in the ongoing profitability of these corporations.

The Global Justice Now report describes this as a corporate merry-go-round where the BMGF consistently acts in the interests of corporations, and cites the following in support of its claim:

- Sue Desmond-Hellmann, BMGF's CEO, spent 14 years at Genentech, a leading health biotechnology company, and was subsequently Chancellor of the University of California at San Francisco, where she 'supported the creation of research partnerships with industry leaders such as Pfizer and Bayer'.
- Leigh Morgan, Chief Operating Officer (COO) at BMGF, previously worked at GlaxoSmithKline and Genentech.
- Emilio Emini joined BMGF in 2015 as Director of HIV program from a position as Chief Scientific Officer and Senior Vice President of Vaccine Research and Development at Pfizer. While at Pfizer, he was already 'a senior advisor to the Gates Foundation's HIV team'. Previously, Emini was the founding Executive Director of Merck's Department of Antiviral Research and the Vice President of Merck's Vaccine and Biologics Research.
- Keith Chirgwin, Deputy Director of Regulatory Affairs at the BMGF, was previously Vice President at Merck Research Labs.
- Penny Heato, who leads Vaccine Development at the BMGF, was previously Global Head of Clinical Research and Development Clusters for Novartis Vaccines and Diagnostics, and Senior Director of Vaccines Clinical Research at Merck Research Laboratories.
- Trevor Mundel, President of Global Health at BMGF, who leads the Foundation's Research and Development-Health, Vaccines and Drugs, was previously involved in clinical research at Pfizer.

The Foundation's agriculture and communications work is largely led by former corporate executives from agribusiness:

- Rob Horsch, who leads the Agricultural Research and Development team, worked at Monsanto for 25 years prior to joining the BMGF.
- Sam Dryden, head of Agricultural Development at the BMGF, previously worked for Monsanto, Union Carbide (where he helped establish Dow AgroSciences, one of the world's largest GM crop companies) and headed two of the world's largest GM seed companies. He was also CEO of Emergent Genetics, the US's third largest cotton seed company, which was sold to Monsanto in 2005. [Dryden passed away in 2017.]
- Miguel Veiga-Pestana, Chief Communications Officer at the BMGF, previously served as Vice-President, Global Sustainability Strategy and External Advocacy at Unilever. [Pestana has moved on from BMGF.]

Other corporations in which the Gates Foundation has invested (as of 2014, cited in the Global Justice Now report) are the mining companies, Barrick Gold, BHP Billiton, Freeport-McMoRan, Glencore, Rio Tinto, Vale and Vedanta. In India, Vedanta has been trying to mine bauxite in the Niyamgiri Hills of the Dongariya Gonds. So far, the tribals have succeeded in protecting their sacred mountain.

As per a report in *The Guardian*, the BMGF has investments in coal giants, Anglo American, BHP Billiton, Glencore Xstrata and Peabody Energy, and in the oil majors Shell, Conoco Phillips, Chevron, Total Petrobras, BP, Anadarko Petroleum. In June 2015, Gates had announced that he would invest $2 billion in renewable energy projects. However, in October 2015, he said that fossil fuel divestment is 'a false solution', and, at the same time, accused environmentalists of making misleading claims about the price of solar power.

The Foundation invests in agribusiness companies Archer Daniels Midland, Kraft, Mondelez International, Nestlé and Unilever. Chemical and pharmaceutical corporations with Gates investments include BASF, Dow Chemicals, GlaxoSmithKline, Novartis and Pfizer; and beverage companies Coca-Cola, Diageo, Pepsico and SABMiller also receive investments from the BMGF. In 2014, Gates had $538 million worth of shares in Coca-Cola. Additionally, the BMGF uses its grants to encourage local communities to partner with Coca-Cola as business affiliates.

As of end-2014, the Foundation had investments worth $852 million in the construction company Caterpillar, which has long been accused of complicity in human rights abuses in the Palestinian Occupied Territories. BAE Systems, the UK's largest arms exporter, is another investee. The Foundation held shares in McDonald's until December 2014, and still holds shares in Arcos Dorados—Latin America's largest quick service chain and the largest McDonald's franchisee in the world, which operates the latter's 2,602 restaurants.

Philanthrocapitalism

The Gates model of philanthrocapitalism has little to do with charity and giving and more to do with profits, control and grabbing. It is, in fact, an economic model of investment and a political model of control, silencing and erasing diversity, democracy and alternatives. New markets and new monopolies are carved out through dominance via aid.

At the 64th World Health Assembly in Geneva on May 16, 2011, Gates admitted that the Foundation funds research in vaccines and, subsequently, takes out patents on them. He said, 'In terms of IP [Intellectual Property], what we do is actually quite simple. We fund research and we actually, ourselves or our partners, create intellectual property so that anything that is invented with our Foundation money that goes to richer countries, we're actually getting a return on that money.'[72]

Gates has given money to fight the Ebola epidemic in Africa, and Gates, the Centers for Disease Control and Prevention (CDC) in Atlanta and the National Institutes of Health (NIH) have patents on the Ebola vaccine. At the G20 Summit in Hamburg, Germany, on July 8, 2017, of all the diseases in the world, Ebola was singled out for attention, indicating just how he sets the 'development' financing agenda.[73]

The Global Justice Now report warns:

Gated Development demonstrates that the trend to involve business in addressing poverty and inequality is central to the priorities and funding of the Bill and Melinda Gates Foundation. We argue that this is a far from neutral charitable strategy but instead an ideological commitment to promote neoliberal economic policies and corporate globalisation. Big business is directly benefitting, in particular in the fields of agriculture and health, as a result of the Foundation's activities, despite evidence to show that business solutions are not the most effective.

Perhaps what is most striking about the Bill and Melinda Gates Foundation is that despite its aggressive corporate strategy and extraordinary influence across governments, academics and the media, there is an absence of critical voices. Global Justice Now is concerned that the Foundation's influence is so pervasive that many actors in international development, which would otherwise critique the policy and practice of the Foundation, are unable to speak out independently as a result of its funding and patronage.

Gated Development further reports, 'A major problem with the focus on technology is that the BMGF, along with other philanthropic foundations, is reshaping aid policy further away from prioritising rights and justice towards a technocratic "authoritarian development"'. For example, Bill Gates, in his 2015 annual letter, stated that the next fifteen years will see major breakthroughs in poor countries which 'will be driven by innovation in technology—ranging from new vaccines and hardier crops to much cheaper smartphones and tablets—and by innovations that help deliver those things to more people'.

One History: an illusion constructed by the 1%

Everything faded into mist. The past was erased, the erasure was forgotten, the lie became truth.

—George Orwell

The struggle of people against power is the struggle of memory against forgetting.

—Milan Kundera

Engineering erasure is a vital element in the creation of the money machine and the delusion of democracy that helps maintain it. This includes the erasures of our diverse knowledges, our diverse economies, our diverse democracies, and our diverse histories. It simultaneously leads to the erasure of the potential of our diversities to coexist in mutual interdependence and cooperation, contributing to a shared prosperity and the common good. It is also an erasure of the violence of colonisation, past and present. The violence is 'naturalised' as progress, and the erasure present at every stage of colonisation as 'creation'. It erases the link between the wealth and power of the coloniser and the poverty and marginalisation of the colonised.

'Development' is part of this narrative, based on Rostow's 'stages of growth' that naturalised the poverty created by colonialism into 'underdevelopment' and offered further colonisation through externally controlled and externally driven 'development' as the solution to that poverty.

Rogue ventures

Among the most irresponsible experiments that Gates is pushing is that of geoengineering, which began as a military tool for weather modification and was part of geopolitical warfare. It is the deliberate modification of weather and climate to intervene in the earth's climate system. Techniques include solar radiation management (SRM), as well as other earth system interventions under the umbrella of carbon dioxide removal (CDR) or greenhouse gas removal (GGR).

Gates and other billionaires are both financing geoengineering experiments and lobbying with governments to back these experiments on a global scale. As per a report in *The Guardian*, in 2009-10, the US government received requests for over $2 billion grants for geoengineering research, but spent around $100 million.[74]

The report states that Professors David Keith of Harvard University and Ken Caldeira of Stanford University received over $4.6 million from Gates to run the Fund for Innovative Climate and Energy Research (FICER). It further adds that according to statements of financial interests, Prof. Keith receives an undisclosed sum from Bill Gates each year, and is the president and majority owner of the geoengineering company Carbon Engineering, incorporated in 2009, in which Gates and another private investor, Murray Edwards, have major stakes—believed to be together worth over $10 million. Another Edwards company, *The Guardian* elaborates, the Canadian Natural Resources, has plans to spend $25 billion to turn the bitumen-bearing sand found in northern Alberta into barrels of crude oil. Caldeira says he receives $375,000 a year from Gates, holds a carbon capture patent and works for Intellectual Ventures, a private geoengineering research company part-owned by Gates and run by Nathan Myhrvold, former head of technology at Microsoft.

As Diana Bronson of ETC (Action Group on Erosion, Technology and Concentration) says in *The Guardian*,

> There are clear conflicts of interest between many of the people involved in the debate. What is really worrying is that the same small group working on high-risk technologies that will geoengineer the planet is also trying to engineer the discussion around international rules and regulations. We cannot put the fox in charge of the chicken coop.

Clive Hamilton, Professor of Public Ethics at the Centre for Applied Philosophy and Public Ethics at Charles Stuart University, and author of *Earthmasters: The Dawn of the Age of Climate Engineering* writes in his blog for *The Guardian*,

> The eco-clique are lobbying for a huge injection of public funds into geoengineering research. They dominate virtually every inquiry into geoengineering. They are present in almost all of the expert deliberations. They have been the leading advisers to parliamentary

and congressional inquiries and their views will, in all likelihood, dominate the deliberations of the UN's Intergovernmental Panel on Climate Change (IPCC) as it grapples for the first time with the scientific and ethical tangle that is climate engineering.

Bill Gates has directed at least $4.5 million of his own money towards the study of methods that could alter the stratosphere by reflecting solar energy, and brightening ocean clouds. Intellectual Ventures has applied for patents on techniques to geoengineer the stratosphere. Along with officials from that organisation, Gates applied for a patent in 2008 to sap hurricanes of their strength by mixing surface and deep ocean water.

Gated Development reports, 'A recent report by *The Lancet* and University College London concluded that climate change is "the biggest global health threat of the 21st century"'. Instead of focusing on pollution and the anthropogenic factors driving climate change, the assumption is that the problem of climate change is that the sun shines on the earth. All geoengineering solutions to climate change are simplistic and non-ecological and focus on blocking the sun, either by reflecting sunlight back through mirrors in the sky or creating artificial volcanoes, or spraying aerosols. But the sun is not the problem. Fossil fuels and the fossil fuel-based industrial system, including industrial agriculture, are the problems. The sun is essential, for without it there would be no photosysthesis, no life, no food.

Climate change is not just global warming, to which the mechanical response is 'global cooling' by life-destroying geoengineering experiments. Climate change is a disruption of the earth's processes through which she regulates the climate. The consequence of this disruption is climate chaos and extreme and unpredictable events. Geoengineering will only aggravate this disruption.

In a paper delivered at a geoengineering conference on ethics, Jane Long (director-at-large for the Lawrence Livermore National Laboratory in the US), cautions, 'We will need to protect ourselves from vested interests [and] be sure that choices are not influenced by parties who might make significant amounts of money through a choice to modify climate, especially using proprietary intellectual property.'[75]

When our age is referred to as the Anthropocene, it refers to the power of man to disrupt the earth's ecological processes. But it would be arrogant and irresponsible to claim that this power to destroy gives some privileged humans the right to commandeer the earth's resources, processes and systems, in denial of the creativity, self-organisation, and diversity of living beings and living systems. Nature is more than a human construct, or an object of human manipulation for short-term benefit; it is the creative force of the universe. To be alive is to live in the Ecocene.

I refer to the Ecocene as both the ecological process of the earth and the biosphere that shapes, maintains and sustains life, and the increasing consciousness among humans, that we are earth citizens, part of the earth community. It includes the awareness that the earth has rights, and that we have a duty to care for her, her creatures, and our fellow humans. And it includes correcting and transcending the mistakes, false assumptions and limitations of the one mechanical mind.

I have consciously avoided calling our times the age of the Anthropocene, because an anthropocentric worldview has caused much of the ecological destruction of our times. To continue putting humans at the centre of consciousness, is to perpetuate human hubris. Moreover, anthropocentrism goes hand in hand with ethnocentrism and the paradigms that emerged in the West with the rise of colonialism, industrialism and capitalism. The rule of the 1% is a hyper anthropocentrism which does not just exclude the rights of all non-human beings, it also excludes most human beings themselves.

The 2017 World Environment Day was dominated by US President Donald Trump walking out of the Paris agreement. What does Trump's arrogance imply for international obligations to protect the earth, for a future based on ecological justice, for sowing the seeds of earth democracy? Environmental laws at the national level were created in the 1970s to protect the earth from harm, and because we live on earth, to protect people from harm.

In 1992, at the Earth Summit in Rio de Janeiro, the international community adopted two major ecological principles—the Precautionary Principle and the Polluter Pays Principle, and signed two legally binding agreements: the CBD and UN Framework Convention on Climate Change (UNFCC).

Both treaties were shaped by emerging ecological sciences and the deepening ecology movement. One was a scientific response to the ecological pollution due to fossil fuels. The second was a scientific response to the genetic pollution caused by GMOs and the erosion of biodiversity due to the spread of industrial, chemical monocultures. Three years after Rio, the UN Leipzig Conference on Plant Genetic Resources assessed that 75 per cent biodiversity had disappeared because of the Green Revolution and industrial farming. Interdisciplinary science and democratic movements created the momentum for international environmental law. Science and democracy continue to be the forces challenging the terrible threat to the earth because of corporate greed.

In the matter of climate change, the key issue is reducing

emissions and developing strategies for adaptation. In the matter of biodiversity conservation, the key issues are biosafety and the adoption and promotion of practices that conserve biodiversity.

A project which illustrates both the shallowness of Gates' ideas and his will to control nature and society (or have a machine do it for him) is the Big History project, to which he has reportedly contributed $10 million. The project is inspired by videos produced by Australian professor, David Christian, which Gates saw while exercising on his treadmill. Christian's videos are not about history, they are about displacing people's histories to create a linear, technocratic vision for a society based on genetic determinism. There are no people in Christian's rendering of history, no cultures, no colonisation, no corporations, no billionaires running an economy for the 1%. Big History is nothing more than a mechanistic, reductionist, technocratic narrative of power and control. It is a story to create a future of the 1%, by the 1%, for the 1%. It is the rewriting of history for Big Money. As Katherine Edwards writes in her article, 'Why the Big History Project is Funded by Bill Gates',[76]

> ... the most alarming aspect of this is not the substance of what Gates and Christian are proposing, it is the fact that someone with no background in history or in education can happen to chance upon an idea one morning while on his treadmill and before long the education of thousands of children is disrupted to align with his latest fad—all because of the enormous economic power he wields.
>
> In the UK, state education is rapidly following the US model, becoming ever more commercialised and divorced from democratic accountability. Local authority schools are being offered bribes by brokers to become academies and the Department for Education has refused to rule out for-profit state schools. We have recently

endured an education secretary who drafted the history curriculum on a whim. Perhaps next time it will be an unelected billionaire.

Bill Gates has an extremely limited vocabulary—of 'innovation', 'technology', and 'investment'. It reveals how his imagination is shaped by the tools of power and control, money and technology.

Multiple voices and messages are at the heart of freedom and democracy. When people are free, they have a voice. When societies are democratic, their voices are heard. When societies become undemocratic, voices are suppressed and silenced. Big Money is threatening democracy by silencing people's diverse voices, controlling and manipulating the message, the medium, and consequently the public mind. One History is also the rewriting of history, of the fabrication of reality, the silencing of the real voices of real people, to create an echo chamber for a genetically engineered, digitally driven narrative.

The Gates story of the 1% is not a universal story

There is no word on ecology and ecosystems in Bill Gates' Universe Story, there is only a project for mastery and control through genetic engineering based on reductionism, geoengineering, and the engineering of history.

Eco-apartheid, the illusion of our separation from nature, is the old story of the mechanistic age; Big History continues this violent separation. We need the birth of the Ecocene, or what F. Thomas Berry calls 'the Ecozoic age', where we recognise that we are earth citizens, members of the earth community. This is the new story that a resurgent humanity is writing by breaking free of fossil fuels, GMOs, and the cages and prisons of mechanistic reductionism; breaking free of the mechanical mind, the money machine, and the pseudo democracy run by the money machine which is robbing us of our histories and our freedoms, our self-organisation and our future. Our futures and freedoms depend on our diverse stories. The colonisation by the 1% depends on erasing our stories, our collective memory, our imagination, from which arise our actions and struggles. People across the world are writing a new story, recognising the brutality of colonisation old and new, exploring new ways of joining the local with the planetary, linking the many creation stories of our diverse cultures, and joining our creativity and intelligence with the creativity and intelligence of every living being. It is the emerging story of one humanity on one planet, refusing to be colonised, resolute in the defence of our diverse, interconnected freedoms.

The Technology Machine of the 1%

Toxic Cartel Shareholders [77]

E.I. du Pont de Nemours & Co.

Name	Equities	%
Capital Research & Management Co. (World Investors)	8,98,38,822	10.3%
The Vanguard Group, Inc.	5,27,55,202	6.05%
SSGA Funds Management, Inc.	3,87,89,007	4.45%
BlackRock Fund Advisors	3,36,22,081	3.86%
Trian Fund Management, LP	2,02,24,075	2.32%
T. Rowe Price Associates, Inc.	1,91,09,105	2.19%
Fidelity Management & Research Co.	1,89,60,764	2.18%
Highfields Capital Management, LP	1,26,20,256	1.45%
Northern Trust Investments, Inc.	1,13,66,263	1.30%
DuPont Capital Management Corp.	99,69,322	1.14%

The Dow Chemical Co.

Name	Equities	%
The Vanguard Group, Inc.	7,05,16,634	6.31%
SSGA Funds Management, Inc.	4,40,53,093	3.94%
BlackRock Fund Advisors	4,20,62,990	3.77%
Capital Research & Management Co. (World Investors)	3,28,79,668	2.94%
Third Point, LLC	2,52,50,000	2.26%
Capital Research & Management Co. (Global Investors)	1,63,65,000	1.46%
Wellington Management Co. LLP	1,36,75,361	1.22%
Northern Trust Investments, Inc.	1,33,13,627	1.19%
Capital Research & Management Co. (International Investors)	1,26,24,713	1.13%
Franklin Advisers, Inc.	1,25,95,870	1.13%

Monsanto Co.

Name	Equities	%
Capital Research & Management Co. (Global Investors)	3,00,09,458	6.81%
The Vanguard Group, Inc.	2,92,53,433	6.64%
SSGA Funds Management, Inc.	1,84,49,843	4.19%
BlackRock Fund Advisors	1,69,38,069	3.85%
Massachusetts Financial Services Co.	1,43,19,095	3.25%
Glenview Capital Management, LLC	1,40,78,428	3.20%
Fidelity Management & Research Co.	1,34,54,547	3.06%
Sands Capital Management, LLC	1,18,54,253	2.69%
PRIMECAP Management Co.	1,16,30,397	2.64%
Davis Selected Advisers LP	82,33,266	1.87%

Syngenta AG

Name	Equities	%
The Vanguard Group, Inc.	17,95,568	1.93%
Norges Bank Investment Management	16,76,873	1.80%
Northern Cross, LLC	16,52,177	1.78%
Jupiter Asset Management Ltd.	16,44,440	1.77%
Fidelity Management & Research Co.	15,80,300	1.70%
UBS AG (Investment Management)	14,58,502	1.57%
Artisan Partners LP	14,23,007	1.53%
Credit Suisse Group AG	12,57,852	1.35%
Capital Research & Management Co. (World Investors)	12,19,000	1.31%
Syngenta AG	11,57,146	1.25%

The Technology Machine of the 1%

Bayer AG

Name	Equities	%
Capital Research & Management Co. (World Investors)	1,93,08,166	2.33%
The Vanguard Group, Inc.	1,67,22,949	2.02%
Lyxor International Asset Management SAS	1,58,28,584	1.91%
Norges Bank Investment Management	1,41,00,744	1.71%
State Street Global Advisors Ltd.	1,39,90,546	1.69%
BlackRock Fund Advisors	1,33,99,616	1.62%
Massachusetts Financial Services Co.	1,30,24,482	1.58%
BlackRock Asset Management Deutschland AG	1,24,04,565	1.50%
Amundi Asset Management SA (Investment Management)	1,00,21,629	1.21%
Dodge & Cox	87,18,170	1.05%

Potash Corp. of Saskatchewan, Inc.

Name	Equities	%
RBC Global Asset Management, Inc.	5,10,34,808	6.10%
Fiduciary Management, Inc.	3,24,26,519	3.87%
First Eagle Investment Management LLC	2,90,74,788	3.47%
Capital Research & Management Co. (World Investors)	2,35,29,769	2.81%
Capital Research & Management Co. (Global Investors)	1,57,71,000	1.88%
Capital Research & Management Co. (Int'l Investors)	1,53,18,560	1.83%
The Vanguard Group, Inc.	1,30,85,152	1.56%
Fidelity Management & Research Co.	1,29,11,995	1.54%
TD Asset Management, Inc.	1,28,07,452	1.53%
CIBC World Markets, Inc.	1,21,55,726	1.45%

Sumitomo Chemical Co., Ltd.

Name	Equities	%
Sumitomo Life Insurance Co.	7,10,00,000	4.29%
Marathon Asset Management LLP	6,59,74,000	3.99%
Nippon Life Insurance Co.	4,10,31,000	2.48%
Sumitomo Mitsui Financial Group, Inc.	3,84,53,000	2.32%
Nomura Asset Management Co., Ltd.	3,37,42,361	2.04%
Sumitomo Life Insurance Pension Fund	2,90,00,000	1.75%
The Vanguard Group, Inc.	2,78,00,990	1.68%
Japan Agricultural Cooperatives	2,18,25,000	1.32%
BlackRock Fund Advisors	2,10,80,000	1.27%
Norges Bank Investment Management	2,09,09,280	1.26%

Akzo Nobel N.V.

Name	Equities	%
Causeway Capital Management, LLC	1,61,38,607	6.52%
Massachusetts Financial Services Co.	1,27,65,488	5.16%
Dodge & Cox	72,63,401	2.93%
The Vanguard Group, Inc.	50,12,124	2.02%
UBS Asset Management (UK) Ltd.	47,94,611	1.94%
Templeton Global Advisors Ltd.	42,60,470	1.72%
Norges Bank Investment Management	39,42,002	1.59%
BlackRock Investment Management, LLC	33,77,093	1.36%
BlackRock Fund Advisors	28,96,876	1.17%
Capital Research & Management Co. (Global Investors)	28,82,000	1.16%

The Technology Machine of the 1%

3M Co.

Name	Equities	%
SSGA Funds Management, Inc.	4,52,51,374	7.47%
The Vanguard Group, Inc.	4,06,26,344	6.71%
BlackRock Fund Advisors	2,39,91,424	3.96%
Massachusetts Financial Services Co.	1,72,24,573	2.84%
State Farm Investment Management Corp.	1,11,31,700	1.84%
Northern Trust Investments, Inc.	86,15,287	1.42%
Fidelity Management & Research Co.	85,55,801	1.41%
First Eagle Investment Management, LLC	62,52,458	1.03%
Norges Bank Investment Management	58,58,227	0.97%
U.S. Bancorp Asset Management, Inc.	55,75,819	0.92%

Intrepid Potash, Inc.

Name	Equities	%
Bayer AG		
Capital Research & Management Co. (Global Investors)	1,93,08,166	2.33%
The Vanguard Group, Inc.	1,67,22,949	2.02%
Lyxor International Asset Management SAS	1,58,28,584	1.91%
Norges Bank Investment Management	1,41,00,744	1.71%
State Street Global Advisors Ltd.	1,39,90,546	1.69%
BlackRock Fund Advisors	1,33,99,616	1.62%
Massachusetts Financial Services Co.	1,30,24,482	1.58%
BlackRock Asset Management Deutschland AG	1,24,04,565	1.50%
Amundi Asset Management SA (Investment Management)	1,00,21,629	1.21%
Dodge & Cox	87,18,170	1.05%

BASF Corporation

Name	Equities	%
The Vanguard Group, Inc. as of 31 Mar 2016	1.80m	1.93%
Norges Bank Investment Management as of 31 Dec 2015	1.68m	1.80%
Northern Cross, LLC as of 31 Jan 2016	1.65m	1.78%
Fidelity Management & Research Co. as of 29 Feb 2016	1.65m	1.78%
Capital Research & Management Co. (Global Investors) as of 31 Jan 2016	1.65m	1.77%
Jupiter Asset Management Ltd. as of 29 Jan 2016	1.64m	1.77%
UBS AG (Investment Management) as of 05 Apr 2016	1.46m	1.57%
Artisan Partners LP as of 31 Mar 2016	1.42m	1.53%
Credit Suisse Group AG as of 07 Apr 2016	1.26m	1.35%
Capital Research & Management Co. (World Investors) as of 31 Dec 2015	1.22m	1.31%

The Technology Machine of the 1%

Endnotes

[1] Rosemary A. Mason, 'The sixth mass extinction and chemicals in the environment: our environmental deficit is now beyond nature's ability to regenerate', *Journal of Biological Physics and Chemistry.* 15, 3 (2015), pp. 160-176; http://www.moraybeedinosaurs.co.uk/neonicotinoid/The_sixth_mass_extinction_and_chemicals_in_the_environment.pdf.

[2] Sanjeeb Mukherjee, 'Big rise in farmer suicides in four states during 2016, says NCRB data', *Business Standard.* http://www.business-standard.com/article/economy-policy/big-rise-in-farmer-suicides-in-four-states-during-2016-says-ncrb-data-118032300025_1.html. Published on March 23, 2018; Deeptiman Tiwary, 'In 80%.farmer-suicides due to debt, loans from banks, not moneylenders', *The Indian Express.* http://www.indianexpress.com. article/india/in-80-farmer-sucides-due-to-debt-loans-from-banks-not-moneylenders-4462930/. Published on January 7, 2017. See also, D. Basu, D. Das, K. Misra, 'Farmer Suicides in India', *Economic & Political Weekly.* 51,21 (2016).

[3] 'Report of the Special Rapporteur on the right to food', 2017. https://documents-dds-ny.un.org/doc/UNDOC/GEN/G17/017/85/PDF/G1701785.pdf?OpenElement.

[4] '"Getting along with their own business": The secret pact of Standard Oil with the Nazis and why Adolf Eichmann was silenced', https://www.gabyweber.com/dwnld/artikel/eichmann/ingles/secret_pact_standard_oil.pdf.

[5] 'The Treason Of Rockefeller Standard Oil (Exxon) During World War II', *The American Chronicle.* https://archive.org/stream/pdfy-eQ-GW5bGFH1vHYJH/The%20Treason%20Of%20Rockefeller%20Standard%20Oil%20(Exxon)%20During%20World%20War%20II_djvu.txt. Published on February 4, 2012.

[6] Report of the Investigation of I.G. Farbenindustrie A.G., prepared by Division of Investigation of Cartels and External Assets, Office of Military Government, U.S. [Germany], November 1945. http://www.markswatson.com/article-IG-Farben-investigation-1945.pdf.

[7] Mira Wilkins, *The History of Foreign Investment in the United States, 1914-1945.* Massachusettes: Harvard University Press, 2009; https://books.google.co.in/books?isbn=0674045181.

[8] 'The I.G. Farben Case', *Nuernberg Military Tribunal Volume VIII*, p. 1286. https://www.phdn.org/archives/www.mazal.org/archive/nmt/08/NMT08-T1286.htm.

[9] Michael A. Whitehouse, 'Paul Warburg's Crusade to Establish a Central Bank in the United States', *The Region*. https://www.minneapolisfed.org/publications/the-region/paul-warburgs-crusade-to-establish-a-central-bank-in-the-united-states. Published on May 1, 1989.

[10] 'The history of "business in diseases"', http://www4.drrathfoundation.org/PHARMACEUTICAL_BUSINESS/history_of_the_pharmaceutical_industry.htm; 'IG Farben: Pharmaceutical Conglomerate (1916 to 2015)', http://www.truthwiki.org/ig-farben-pharmaceutical-conglomerate-1916-to-2015/.

[11] Steven MacMillan, 'Bayer and Monsanto: A Marriage Made in Hell', *New Easter Outlook*. https://journal-neo.org/2016/05/21/bayer-and-monsanto-a-marriage-made-in-hell/. Published on May 21, 2016.

[12] 'A Bayer-Monsanto merger would violate anti-trust laws to create the largest agroindustrial company in the world', https://www.bayermonsantomerger.com; 'Here's How a Bayer-Monsanto Merger Affects Workers, Farmers, and Investors', *Fortune.com*, http://fortune.com/2016/05/24/bayer-monsanto-merger/. Published on May 24, 2016; Deidre Fulton, 'Bayer-Monsanto Merger Is "Five-Alarm Threat" to Food and Farms: Legal Experts', *Common Dreams*, http://www.commondreams.org/news/2016/08/03/bayer-monsanto-merger-five-alarm-threat-food-and-farms-legal-experts. Published on August 3, 2016; Francesco Canepa, 'Bayer could get ECB financing for Monsanto bid, rules show', *Reuters.com*, http://www.reuters.com/article/us-monsanto-bayer-ecb-idUSKCN0YG2G9. Published on May 25, 2016.

[13] 'Monsanto Tribunal And People's Assembly', *Seedfreedom.info*. http://seedfreedom.info/campaign/international-monsanto-tribunal/.

[14] 'Mergers: Commission clears Bayer's acquisition of Monsanto, subject to conditions', European Commission press release database. http://europa.eu/rapid/press-release_IP-18-2282_en.htm. Published on March 21, 2018.

[15] 'People's Assembly on Dow-Dupont Crimes of Genocide and Ecocide', *Seedfreedom.info*. https://seedfreedom.info/peoples-assembly-on-dow-dupont-crimes-of-genocide-and-ecocide/. Published on November 21, 2016.

[16] '"Bayer-Monsanto: Get-Off Our Plates!" Town hall meeting', *Seedfreedom.*

info. https://seedfreedom.info/events/bayer-monsanto-get-off-our-plates-town-hall-meeting/.

[17] Amit Sen Gupta, 'Bayer Sues Indian Government to Retain Monopoly Right', *Political Affairs.* http://www.politicalaffairs.net/bayer-sues-indian-government-to-retain-monopoly-right/. Published on February 10, 2009.

[18] Chris Neiger, 'A $3 Trillion Market in 2020: 3 Sectors You Need to Watch', *The Motley Fool,* https://www.fool.com/investing/general/2016/04/17/a-3-trillion-market-in-2020-3-sectors-you-need-t-2.aspx. Published on Aril 17, 2016. See also, 'Monsanto to Acquire The Climate Corporation, Combination to Provide Farmers with Broad Suite of Tools Offering Greater On-Farm Insights', https://monsanto.com/news-releases/monsanto-to-acquire-the-climate-corporation-combination-to-provide-farmers-with-broad-suite-of-tools-offering-greater-on-farm-insights/. Published on October 2, 2013; and 'The Climate Corporation Announces Acquisition of Soil Analysis Business Line of Solum Inc.', https://climate.com/newsroom/climate-corp-acquires-soil-analysis-business-line/2. Published on February 20, 2014.

[19] Lily Kay, *The Molecular Vision of Life.* Oxford: Oxford University Press, 1992, p. 8.

[20] Ibid, p. 27.

[21] Ibid. p. 27, 34.

[22] Kay, op. cit.

[23] Richard C. Lewontin, *Biology as Ideology: The Doctrine of DNA.* London: Penguin Books, 1991.

[24] Carl R. Woese, 'A New Biology for a New Century', *Microbiology And Molecular Biology Reviews.* 68, 2 (2004), pp. 173–186. http://mmbr.asm.org/content/68/2/173.full.

[25] 'Seeds of Suicide', Research Foundation for Science, Technology and Ecology (RFSTE), 1999.

[26] RFSTE, Navdanya's fieldwork in Vidarbha and an analysis of National Crime Records Bureau (NCRB) state data on suicides in the Bt cotton growing region.

[27] Peng Wan, Yunxin Huang, Huaiheng Wu, Minsong Huang, Shengbo Cong, et. al., 'Increased Frequency of Pink Bollworm Resistance to Bt Toxin Cry1Ac in China'. *PLOS ONE.* 7, 1 (2012), e29975. http://journals.plos.org/plosone/article?id=10.1371/journal.pone.0029975; Bruce E. Tabashnik, Thierry

Brévault and Yves Carrière, 'Insect Resistance to Bt crops: Lessons from the First Billion Acres'. *Nature Biotechnology*. 31, (2013), pp. 510–521. http://www. nature.com/nbt/journal/v31/n6/abs/nbt.2597.html?foxtrotcallback=true; https://ucanr.edu/repositoryfiles/ca5206p14-67769.pdf.

[28] Pavan Dahat, '9 farmers die in Yavatmal after spraying insecticide on crops', *The Hindu*. http://www.thehindu.com/news/national/other-states/9-farmers-die-in-yavatmal-after-spraying-insecticide-on-crops/article19758683.ece. Published on September 26, 2017.

[29] Priyanka Kakodkar and Bhavika Jain, 'Pesticide toll at 35, Maharashtra forms SIT', *The Times of India*. https://timesofindia.indiatimes.com/city/mumbai/pesticide-toll-at-35-maharashtra-forms-sit/articleshow/61029909. cms. Published on October 11, 2017.

[30] Priyanka Kakodkar and Bhavika Jain, 'SIT to probe 35 Vidarbha pesticide deaths, FIR filed against agro firm', *The Times of India*. https://timesofindia. indiatimes.com/city/mumbai/sit-to-probe-35-vidarbha-pesticide-deaths-fir-filed-against-agro-firm/articleshow/61028959.cms. Published on October 11, 2017 ; 'Devendra Fadnavis orders SIT probe into farmer deaths due to pesticides poisoning in Vidarbha; agro firm booked', *First Post*. http://www. firstpost.com/india/devendra-fadnavis-orders-sit-probe-into-farmer-deaths-due-to-pesticides-poisoning-in-vidarbha-agro-firm-booked-4132025.html. Published on October 11, 2017; Swapnil Rawal, 'Pesticides kill 28 farmers: Maharashtra government orders third probe', *Hindustan Times*. http://www. hindustantimes.com/mumbai-news/pesticides-kill-28-farmers-maharashtra-government-orders-third-probe/story-lpBFnJnlx9spPfFSqfRVdO.html. Published on October 11, 2017; Bhavika Jain, Mazhar Ali, Shakti Singh and Priyanka Kakodkar, 'CM orders SIT to probe pesticide deaths in Vid', *The Times of India*. https://timesofindia.indiatimes.com/city/nagpur/cm-orders-sit-to-probe-pesticide-deaths-in-vid/articleshow/61028159.cms. Published on October 11, 2017.

[31] Mayank Bhardwaj, 'Andhra Pradesh revokes order to check planting of Monsanto GM cotton', *Reuters*. http://in.reuters.com/article/india-monsanto-cotton-andhrapradesh/andhra-pradesh-revokes-order-to-check-planting-of-monsanto-gm-cotton-idINKBN1CJ0HD?utm_campaign=true Anthem:+Trending+Content&utm_content=59e2199004d3014fb286eacf &utm_medium=trueAnthem&utm_source=twitter. Published on October 14, 2017.

[32] 'The Toxic Story of Roundup: Freedom from the Poison Cartel through Agroecology', Navdanya, 2017. http://seedfreedom.info/wp-content/uploads/2017/09/The-Toxic-Story-of-RoundUp.pdf.

[33] Ruchi Shroff, 'New Study Shows Glyphosate Contaminates Soils - Half of Europe At Risk', Navdanya. https://www.navdanyainternational.it/en/news-navdanya-international/464-glyphosate-contaminates-soils. Published on October 19, 2017; 'High levels of glyphosate in agricultural soil: "Extension of approval not prudent."', Wageningen University & Research. https://www.wur.nl/en/newsarticle/High-levels-of-glyphosate-in-agricultural-soil-Extension-of-approval-not-prudent.-.htm. Published on October 16, 2017.

[34] Kathryn Z. Guyton, et. all., 'Carcinogenicity of tetrachlorvinphos, parathion, malathion, diazinon, and glyphosate', The Lancet Oncology. 16, 5 (2015), pp. 490-491; http://www.thelancet.com/journals/lanonc/article/PIIS1470-2045(15)70134-8/abstract.

[35] James Corbett, 'Court Documents Reveal the Inner Workings of a Monsanto Smear Campaign', Steemit.com. https://steemit.com/news/@corbettreport/court-documents-reveal-the-inner-workings-of-a-monsanto-smear-campaign. Published on August 5, 2017.

[36] Helmut Burtscher-Schaden, Peter Clausing and Claire Robinson, 'Glyphosate and cancer: Buying science', GLOBAL 2000. https://www.global2000.at/sites/global/files/Glyphosate_and_cancer_Buying_science_EN_0.pdf. Published in March 2017; Cary Gillam, 'New "Monsanto Papers" Add To Questions Of Regulatory Collusion, Scientific Mischief', Huffington Post.com. https://www.huffingtonpost.com/entry/newly-released-monsanto-papers-add-to-questions-of_us_597fc800e4b0d187a5968fbf. Published on August 1, 2017; 'The Monsanto Papers: Roundup (Glyphosate) Cancer Case Key Documents & Analysis', U.S. Right to Know (USRTK). https://usrtk.org/pesticides/mdl-monsanto-glyphosate-cancer-case-key-documents-analysis/; Jennifer Sass, 'European Parliament Takes Aim at Monsanto and Glyphosate', NRDC. https://www.nrdc.org/experts/jennifer-sass/european-parliament-takes-aim-monsanto-and-glyphosate. Published on October 9, 2017.

[37] Liz Gannes, 'Silicon Valley Big-Data Startup Bought for $1B by... Monsanto?', All Things Digital. http://allthingsd.com/20131002/silicon-valley-big-data-startup-bought-for-1b-by-monsanto/. Published on

October 2, 2013; 'The Climate Corporation Announces Acquisition of Soil Analysis Business Line of Solum, Inc.', https://monsanto.com/news-releases/the-climate-corporation-announces-acquisition-of-soil-analysis-business-line-of-solum-inc/. Published on February 20, 2014.

[38] See, https://climate.com/.

[39] Greg Trotter, 'What Monsanto's venture capital group has in common with the CIA', *Chicago Tribune*. http://www.chicagotribune.com/business/ct-monsanto-growth-ventures-1209-biz-20161209-story.html. Published on December 9, 2016.

[40] Amanda Little, 'This Silicon Valley hotshot is modernizing one of the world's most conservative industries', *Grist*. http://grist.org/article/this-silicon-valley-hotshot-is-modernizing-one-of-the-worlds-most-conservative-industries/? utm_source=syndication&utm_medium=rss&utm_campaign=feedfood%E 2%80%93grist. Published on February 1, 2016.

[41] Ed Yong, 'The White House Launches the National Microbiome Initiative', *The Atlantic*. https://www.theatlantic.com/science/archive/2016/05/white-house-launches-the-national-microbiome-initiative/482598/. Published on May 13, 2016.

[42] Pope Alexander VI, *Inter caetera* (May 4, 1493). Transcription source: Frances Gardiner Davenport (Ed.), *European Treaties bearing on the History of the United States and its Dependencies to 1648*. Washington, D.C.: Carnegie Institution of Washington, 1917, pp. 61-63.

[43] 'Who is Bill Gates? Microsoft founder, world's richest man and philanthropist', *The Telegraph*. http://www.telegraph.co.uk/technology/0/bill-gates/. Published on August 1, 2017.

[44] Julie Bort, 'This Is The Man Who's Making Bill Gates So Rich', *Business Insider India*. http://www.businessinsider.in/This-Is-The-Man-Whos-Making-Bill-Gates-So-Rich/articleshow/42939699.cms. Published on Spetember 20, 2014.

[45] Michael Miller, 'The Rise of DOS: How Microsoft Got the IBM PC OS Contract', *PC Magazine*. http://in.pcmag.com/opinion/42422/the-rise-of-dos-how-microsoft-got-the-ibm-pc-os-contract. Published on August 11, 2011; John G. Kemeny, Thomas E. Kurtz, *Basic: A Manual for BASIC, the Elementary Algebraic Language Designed For Use With the Dartmouth Time Sharing System*. (PDF, 1st edition). New Hampshire: Dartmouth College Computation

Center, 1964;'Thomas E. Kurtz-History of Computer Programming Languages', cis-alumni.org. Retrieved on June 13, 2017.

[46] Dolia Estevez, 'Bill Gates And Carlos Slim To Partner On Reducing Hunger', *Forbes*. http://www.forbes.com/sites/doliaestevez/2013/02/13/bill-gates-and-carlos-slim-to-partner-on-reducing-hunger/#532c6d5f3049. Published on February 13, 2013.

[47] Glenn Davis Stone and Domonic Glover, 'Disembedding grain: Golden Rice, the Green Revolution, and heirloom seeds in the Philippines', *Journal of the Agriculture, Food, and Human Values Society*. 34, 1 (2017), pp 87-102. http://link.springer.com/article/10.1007/s10460-016-9696-1.

[48] Allison Wilson, 'Goodbye to Golden Rice? GM Trait Leads to Drastic Yield Loss and "Metabolic Meltdown"', *Independent Science News*. https://www.independentsciencenews.org/health/goodbye-golden-rice-gm-trait-leads-to-drastic-yield-loss/. Published on October 25, 2017; 'Nutritious Rice and Cassava Aim to Help Millions Fight Malnutrition | Bill & Melinda Gates Foundation', Bill and Melinda Gates Foundation media release (2011). https://www.gatesfoundation.org/Media-Center/Press-Releases/2011/04/Nutritious-Rice-and-Cassava-Aim-to-Help-Millions-Fight-Malnutrition; 'HarvestPlus Receives US$6 Million Gates Foundation Grant to Disseminate Biofortified Sweetpotato to the Undernourished in Africa', Bill and Melinda Gates Foundation media release (2015). https://www.gatesfoundation.org/Media-Center/Press-Releases/2005/12/HarvestPlus-Nourishes-East-Africa.

[49] Vandana Shiva, 'GE Vitamin "A" Rice: A Blind Approach to Blindness Prevention'. http://www.amberwaves.org/articlePages/articles/shiva/getVitamin.pdf.

[50] Vandana Shiva, 'Women and Biodiversity Feed the World, Not Corporations and GMOs', *Common Dreams*. http://www.commondreams.org/views/2015/05/20/women-and-biodiversity-feed-world-not-corporations-and-gmos. Published on May 20, 2015.

[51] 'Gates Foundation Grants Additional $6.4 million to Cornell's Controversial Alliance for Science', *Independent Science News*. https://www.independentsciencenews.org/news/gates-foundation-grants-additional-6-4million-to-cornells-controversial-alliance-for-science/. Published on November 1, 2017.

[52] *Smart Breeding*, Greenpeace International, November 2009. http://www.

greenpeace.org/eu-unit/Global/eu-unit/reports-briefings/2009/11/smart-breeding.pdf.

[53] http://www.pricklyresearch.com/AutoIndex/index.php?dir=digitalgene banking/&file=DivSeek_Paper_25May2016.pdf.

[54] 'Agricultural Development: Strategy Overview', Bill and Melinda Gates Foundation. http://www.gatesfoundation.org/What-We-Do/Global-Development/Agricultural-Development/Agriculture-Partners.

[55] Matthew Herper, 'Bill Gates And 13 Other Investors Pour $120 Million Into Revolutionary Gene-Editing Startup', *Forbes*. https://www.forbes.com/sites/matthewherper/2015/08/10/bill-gates-and-13-other-investors-pour-120-million-into-revolutionary-gene-editing-startup/#5555ca6f6369. Published on August 10, 2015. See also, 'The Genesis Engine', *Wired*. https://www.wired.com/2015/12/the-genesis-engine/. Published on December 21, 2015.

[56] Kellie A. Schaefer, Wen-Hsuan Wu, Diana F. Colgan, Stephen H. Tsang, Alexander G. Bassuk, and Vinit B. Mahajan, 'Unexpected mutations after CRISPR-Cas9 editing in vivo', *Nature Methods*. 14, 6 (2017), pp. 547-548. doi:10.1038/nmeth.4293.

[57] Franziska Fichtner, Reynel Urrea Castellanos and Bekir Ülker, 'Precision genetic modifications: a new era in molecular biology and crop improvement', *Planta*. 239, 4 (2014), pp. 921-39. https://doi.org/10.1007/s00425-014-2029-y.

[58] Yanfang Fu, Jennifer A. Foden, Cyd Khayter, Morgan L. Maeder, Deepak Reyon, J. Keith Joung and Jeffry D. Sander, 'High-frequency off-target mutagenesis induced by CRISPR-Cas nucleases in human cells', *Nature Biotechnology*. 31, 9 (2013), pp. 822-26. doi: 10.1038/nbt.2623.

[59] Matthew Herper, 'Bill Gates And 13 Other Investors Pour $120 Million Into Revolutionary Gene-Editing Startup', *Forbes*. https://www.forbes.com/sites/matthewherper/2015/08/10/bill-gates-and-13-other-investors-pour-120-million-into-revolutionary-gene-editing-startup/#5555ca6f6369. Published on August 10, 2015.

[60] Sharon Begley, 'CRISPR Patent Fight: The Legal Bills are Soaring', *STAT News*. https://www.statnews.com/2016/08/12/crispr-patent-fight-legal-bills-soaring/. Published on August 16, 2016.

[61] 'Bayer and CRISPR Therapeutics joint venture, named Casebia Therapeutics, establishes operations in Cambridge, MA', Bayer Global media release. http://www.press.bayer.com/baynews/baynews.nsf/id/

Bayer-CRISPR-Therapeutics-joint-venture-named-Casebia-Therapeutics-establishes-operations-Cambridge. Published on August 19, 2016.

[62] John Carroll, 'Bayer bets $335M on CRISPR Therapeutics and the future of gene editing', *Fierce Biotech*. https://www.fiercebiotech.com/partnering/bayer-bets-335m-on-crispr-therapeutics-and-future-of-gene-editing. Published on December 21, 2015.

[63] Andrew Pollack, 'Jennifer Doudna, a Pioneer Who Helped Simplify Genome Editing', *The New York Times*. http://www.nytimes.com/2015/05/12/science/jennifer-doudna-crispr-cas9-genetic-engineering.html?_r=0. Published on May 11, 2015.

[64] 'Monsanto (MON) Enters Global Genome-Editing Licensing Agreement for CRISPR System', *StreetInsider.com*. http://www.streetinsider.com/Corporate+News/Monsanto+(MON)+Enters+Global+Genome-Editing+Licensing+Agreement+for+CRISPR+System/12390427.html. Published on January 4, 2017.

[65] Mahendra Singh, 'Note ban bold, will kill shadow economy: Bill Gates', *The Times of India*. http://timesofindia.indiatimes.com/Note-ban-bold-will-kill-shadow-economy-Bill-Gates/articleshow/55468005.cms. Published on November 17, 2016.

[66] *An Economy For the 1%*, Oxfam International. https://www.oxfam.org/en/research/economy-1. Published on January 18, 2016; *An Economy for the 99%*, Oxfam International. https://www.oxfam.org/en/research/economy-99. Published on January 16, 2017; *Reward Work, Not Wealth*, Oxfam International. https://www.oxfam.org/en/research/reward-work-not-wealth. Published by January 22, 2018.

[67] Charles Pillers, 'How Piracy Opens Doors for Windows', *Los Angeles Times*. http://articles.latimes.com/2006/apr/09/business/fi-micropiracy9. Published on April 9, 2006.

[68] 'A Well-Kept Open Secret: Washington is behind India's Brutal Experiment of Abolishing Most Cash', http://norberthaering.de/en/home/27-german/news/745-washington-s-role-in-india#weiterlesen. Published on January 1, 2017.

[69] 'GST Launch Highlights: President Pranab Mukherjee, PM Modi Launch India's Biggest Tax Reform', *NDTV*. https://www.ndtv.com/india-news/live-gst-launch-2017-government-to-rollout-the-biggest-tax-reform-at-midnight-1718823. Published on July 1, 2017.

70 https://www.microsoft.com/en-in/campaign/microsoft-gst/registration. aspx; Jasmeen Nagpal, 'EasemyGST partners with Microsoft to launch GST compliance solution', Microsoft News Centre India. https://news.microsoft. com/en-in/easemygst-partners-microsoft-launch-gst-compliance-solution/. Published on May 25, 2017; https://mbs.microsoft.com/customersource/ Global/AX/downloads/tax-regulatory-updates/GST-India.
71 Pranbihanga Borpuzari, 'Sun shines for Cloud, but GST can be pivotal for Microsoft', *The Economic Times.* //economictimes.indiatimes. com/articleshow/59572969.cms?utm_source=contentofinterest&utm_ medium=text&utm_campaign=cppst;https://economictimes.indiatimes. com/small-biz/security-tech/technology/sun-shines-for-cloud-but-gst- can-be-pivotal-for-microsoft/articleshow/59572969.cms. Published on July 13, 2017.
72 William New and Catherine Saez, 'Bill Gates Calls For "Vaccine Decade"; Explains How Patent System Drives Public Health Aid', *Intellectual Property Watch.* https://www.ip-watch.org/2011/05/17/bill-gates-calls-for-vaccine- decade-explains-how-patent-system-drives-public-health-aid/. Published on May 17, 2011.
73 'The CDC, NIH & Bill Gates Own the Patents On Existing Ebola & Related Vaccines: Mandatory Vaccinations Are Near', *Thecommonsenseshow. com.* http://www.thecommonsenseshow.com/2014/09/17/the-cdc-nih- bill-gates-own-the-patents-on-existing-ebola-related-vaccines-mandatory- vaccinations-are-near/.
74 John Vidal, 'Bill Gates backs climate scientists lobbying for large- scale geoengineering', *The Guardian.* https://www.theguardian.com/ environment/2012/feb/06/bill-gates-climate-scientists-geoengineering. Published on February 6, 2012.
75 Vidal, op. cit.
76 Katherine Edwards, 'Why the Big History project funded by Bill Gates is alarming', *The Guardian.* http://www.theguardian.com/commentisfree/2014/ sep/10/big-history-bill-gates-uk-state-schools-education. Published on September 10, 2014.
77 Toxic Cartel Shareholder lists, 2016. These figures have been distributed at the Monsanto Tribunal and People's Assembly as well as the Bayer-Monsanto shareholder meetings. Such research is increasingly becoming difficult since there is an erasure of public information from the Internet.

4 How the 1% Subverts Democracy

Humanity stands at an evolutionary crossroads. We can either choose to continue to walk towards our extinction on the path shaped by the 1% over the last 500 years, or we can choose to sow the seeds of the future as members of the earth community, with a consciousness and conviction that extinction is not inevitable, that we have the potential to walk another path shaped by our commitment to peaceful co-evolution with other species and cultures. We will either make peace with the earth and secure our future survival by realising we are on earth and a part of it, or we will face extinction as humans even as we push millions of other species to extinction. We will either make peace with our diversity, or destroy the social fabric woven by diversity, and, with it, destroy the social conditions for our continued existence.

We can consciously choose the path of oneness, living and celebrating our many diversities, interconnected through bonds of compassion, interdependence, and solidarity; or we can, for a short time, live enslaved by the 1%, internalising the powerlessness and marginalisation they engineer, afraid to change, clinging to illusions of security, while our real ecological security is undermined, and our real social security, embodied in real relationships, is ruptured and broken through the politics of division, hate and fear. The choice is between freedom through oneness vs. slavery to the 1%. Between staying alive vs extinction.

The Resurgence of the Real has become a precondition for the continued survival and evolution of our species. Living through illusions is no longer a luxury we can afford. We must become aware that rejuvenating the planet and reclaiming humanity are not two different ends, reached through different paths, because the earth and society are interwoven in one indivisible, vibrant, colourful fabric of life.

How the 1% Subverts Democracy

Breaking free of the the 1% and their constructs is not just possible, it has become necessary. It is an ecological necessity because the worldview of separation combined with an illusion of limitless extraction and exploitation of nature is pushing us to an ecological precipice. It is an economic necessity because a 1% world will render the 99% disposable, extinguishing our diverse creativities, potentials and possibilities. It is a democratic necessity because the rule of the 1% is a violent dictatorship. It destroys our fundamental freedoms, and the freedoms for all beings to evolve in an interrelated world, in an earth family. It is a social necessity because the world of the 1% destroys our social being, our communities, and our commons, through privatisation and enclosure of the commons; by reducing us to being consumers; and dividing us on the basis of gender, race, and religion. It is a human necessity because participating in a world of limitless greed, profit, violence and power robs us of our humanity. Both the 1% rulers and the 99% disposable people lose their humanity. Greed, fear and hate go hand-in-hand, helping each other grow.

Over the past four-and-a-half-decades of work to conserve the earth's resources, on my intellectual journey to transcend the mechanical mind, and my engagement with creating living economies based on non-violence and real creativity; genuine democracies based on real freedom; and living cultures based on love and compassion, I have always turned to India's struggle for freedom from the British Empire, and to Gandhi's teachings, for inspiration to act in times of hopelessness; to open spaces when all spaces are shrinking; to cultivate compassion and solidarity in times of greed, fear and hate; to reclaim our power when we are being told power is the monopoly of those who derive fake power from money, and money alone.

While the times have changed, the patterns of colonisation stay the same, based on violence, the destruction of people's freedoms and economies, taking what is not yours, collecting unjust rents, creating constructs of divide and rule, and of supremacy. The patterns of liberation and freedom are also perennial, and these contours of freedom shape the road to the Resurgence of the Real.

The chains of unfreedom are globally integrated today. They control every dimension of our lives through a consolidated system designed by the mechanical mind and the money machine. The control is exerted through the construction of illusions, through convergence and concentration, through imposing the laws that allow the free operation of the money machine, through banning people's alternatives that are based on real freedom.

Three Gandhian principles that the Mahatma distilled from the struggles and practice of freedom throughout history have been my inspiration—Swaraj: self-organisation, self-rule, freedom as autopoiesis; Swadeshi: self-reliance and creating local economies; and Satyagraha: the force of truth, of creative civil disobedience.

Swaraj—the resurgence of real freedom for all beings

Because we are not isolated, atomised particles, but interconnected beings, freedom is not atomistic. It is relational, and it is interconnected. Human freedom is indivisible from the freedom of the earth and the rights of all her beings. Humans are less free when they destroy nature and nature's rights. Human freedom is a continuum, including the freedom of all colours, faiths, genders, and cultures. Freedom is self-organisation, autopoesis.

150

How the 1% Subverts Democracy

The lack of freedom is manifest in an externally-imposed uniformity, allopoesis.

Swaraj, self-rule, self-governance, is the basis of real freedom in nature and society, beginning at the smallest level and emerging at higher levels, because it allows the thriving of biological and cultural diversity. Swaraj defined India's freedom movement, encompassing not just political freedom, but economic freedom as well. Gandhi's *Hind Swaraj* has been, for me, the best teaching on real freedom in the context of industrialisation and the Empire. It has become even more relevant in the search for freedom in times of corporate rule. Gandhi wrote *Hind Swaraj* in 1909, more than one-hundred years ago, on his way from England to South Africa. It was first published in the columns of *Indian Opinion* in South Africa; in the 1921 edition, he wrote the following as 'A Word of Explanation',

> In my opinion it is a book which can be put into the hands of a child... It teaches the gospel of love in place of that of hate. It replaces violence with self-sacrifice. It puts soul force against brute force...

For Gandhi, true civilisation is that mode of conduct which directs humans onto the path of right livelihood; and based on this concept of right livelihood, he defined freedom: 'It is swaraj when we learn to rule ourselves.' This is autopoesis in the political context.

According to him, a society based on swaraj is a true democracy since it is based on the realisation that people are in charge of their destinies. It is based on lok shakti or people's power. Swaraj involves not just the periodic accountability of government through elections (which, in any case, have been hijacked by Big Money), it implies freedom from domination, coercion and institutionalised violence which is structural to centralised governance.

He believed that 'democracy must in essence mean the art and science of mobilising the entire physical, economic and spiritual resources of all the various sections of the people in the service of the common good for all'. Gandhi was deeply uneasy with the modern state, as it was abstracted from society, centralised, bureaucratic, obsessed with homogeneity, and suffused with the spirit of violence. He believed that since all prevailing forms of government took the modern state for granted and represented different ways of organising it, they were inherently incapable of tackling its structural defects.

The philosophy of participatory, direct democracy and democratic pluralism recognises that diverse communities have diverse interests, that in the shaping of national law and policy they all have legitimate democratic rights of decision-making and self-determination through self-rule. It acknowledges that representative democracy is inadequate for protecting people's interests in an era of globalisation.

Under corporate influence, governments increasingly act on behalf of corporations. Political power today reflects the top 1% of the economic pyramid, crushing the 99%, and with them, the earth and her species. The State is mutating into a corporate entity working for corporate welfare, leaving the people and the planet to suffer the consequences of economic collapse, ecosystem collapse and climate change. Our challenge is to look for ways to shift the dominant political system away from the exploitative and non-sustainable economic model.

The demand for their democratic rights has been expressed by tribal and indigenous peoples as the self-determined right to agricultural biodiversity through their right to plant genetic resources, and the self-determined right to practice sustainable agriculture. In systems that are characterised by the patriarchal domination of women, urban domination over rural areas, and colonisers dominating over indigenous people, democratic pluralism necessarily requires an inclusion of communities that have hitherto been excluded. This would certainly transform both the communities characterised by internal inequalities as well as the governance structures within countries.

The philosophy of democratic pluralism also recognises the anti-democratic nature of the centralised nation state on which State protectionism of the past was founded. At the same time, it sees the emergence of corporate protectionism and of the corporate surveillance state as real threats to democratic rights and economic livelihoods in every country. In this perspective, countering such recolonisation requires the reinvention of national sovereignty by democratic processes, to create national systems which act in partnership with local communities to protect the natural wealth and the intellectual heritage of the country, and the self-organisation by people.

People's movements are demanding that power must not be concentrated in institutions of centralised nation states; it must be distributed equitably throughout society and be dispersed through a multiplicity of institutions, with more power at the local level, controlled by local communities and their institutions. Whereas conventional power moves from centralised control of nation states to the even more centralised control of global corporations and global institutions like the World Trade Organization (WTO), World Bank and the IMF, people's democratically-driven agendas push for greater localisation, both political and economic.

Political localisation means more decisions are transferred to the local space. Political decentralisation and localisation and Gandhi's swaraj imply circular democracies and the circulation of power through society.

Participation is central to this new democracy, an inclusive democracy for all humans—irrespective of class, gender, religion, and race. It goes beyond representation, and is based on daily participation, not simply on a vote once every four or five years. It is based on caring for the land and nature; on participation in, and cultivation of, communities that act with strength and solidarity to protect the earth and society when the erosion of democracy is all around us.

The old democracy, based on electoral representation, is a linear extraction of power from the people. It is increasingly leaving people powerless to protect their land, their lives, their livelihoods, and their freedoms in the face of land grab, the destruction of livelihoods, and the destruction of our life support systems and democratic rights.

We need to sow the seeds of real freedom in our imaginations and in our daily lives, through our everyday actions, and in our diverse and multiple relationships. The seeds of freedom are in our minds and in our hands. Swaraj, as self-organised freedom, begins deep within each of us, allowing for the possibility of cooperation and the cultivation of self-governing communities. It enables a transition from scarcity, competition and fear to the co-creation of abundance through sharing.

The resurgence of the real begins with breaking free of the invisible prisons institutionalised by the 1%, and becoming aware of our interconnectedness with other beings and other human beings, as well as with our own potential to create and produce in partnership with nature and our communities.

The first prison is the mechanical mind which fragments our

worldview, denies our intelligence and creativity, shrinks our potential and our being, and cripples nature and us, reducing both to raw materials for the money machine. Changing how we think about the world is the most important step towards transforming our lives and transforming the world of which we are a part. The resurgence of the real begins with knowing reality through living reality and living intelligence.

The diversity of species calls on us to protect the ecological space and freedom of all species. The 'wild' is the capacity for self-organisation of all life, the diverse species of the earth and the earth herself as a living organism. This is the consciousness that must shape cultures and communities, economies and democracies, sciences and technologies. In the contemporary order, still dominated by the 1%, the earth community has been reduced to the human community. Humans, as earth citizens with duties and rights, have been replaced by corporations, with no duties to either the earth or society, only unlimited rights to exploit both. Corporations have been assigned legal personhood, and corporate rights are now extinguishing the rights of the earth, and the rights of people to the earth's resources.

The major democratic issue emerging in India, and throughout the world, in the context of the destruction unleashed by the money machine, are the rights of the earth and the democratic and human rights of all people, especially the most marginalised and the most vulnerable. And across the world, communities are organising to defend the rights of the earth.

We can no longer afford to create separations and walls between knowledge systems, economic systems and political systems. We can no longer think and act in silos. We need to connect the economy to democracy, and economic democracy to earth democracy. Seeing interconnectedness and making connections is our opening for creating a new world based on freedom for all life to flourish in wellness.

Swaraj, in our times, is earth democracy. Thinking and acting as one humanity is now an economic and political imperative. When we practise earth democracy based on local living democracy, the principle becomes applicable to all societies and all communities. In earth democracy, humans cannot prosper if the earth that nourishes them is being destroyed. In earth democracy, one species cannot exploit or exterminate others; one gender, one race, one religion, of humans cannot become 'great' by denying others the freedom, respect and dignity that are their rights.

People in India and across the world are responding with a new politics of 'localisation' and self-rule. They are engaged in an enlightened response of putting globalisation in its ecological and social context. In region after region, where foreign investment is diverting local resources from the survival needs of local communities to the boundless appetite of global markets, people are putting investment to the test of ecological and social accountability. They are redefining the principles of governance on the basis of decentralised democracy. The rule of the World Bank and the WTO has implied the rule of super-state institutions serving the one-sided interest of commerce and the 1%, beyond and outside the democratic control of people. As the State withdraws from environmental and social regulation in the 'free-trade' era, as environmental and social justice laws are suspended in the name of 'ease of doing business', communities are organising to regulate commercial activity by asserting their democratic right to decide how these resource are used. They are redefining democracy in terms of people's decisions in their everyday lives. They are redefining the nation in terms of the land and the people, rich in their diversity.

The trend towards localisation was, in fact, born at the same time as the trend towards globalisation. If globalisation is the corporate-driven agenda for control, localisation is the countervailing citizens' agenda for protecting the environment and ensuring people's survival and livelihood. In the absence of regulation by national governments, citizens are creating a new politics for introducing ecological limits. Localisation has an inbuilt environmental component for the control and ownership of local resources, a decision-making component for the utilisation of these resources, and an economic component that resists the destruction of local economies by the global economy and international trade.

Movements for localisation are giving rise to a new people's ecological protectionism which is fundamentally different from corporate protectionism in which all institutions of society courts, the police and government departments—are distorted to protect the interests of transnational corporations (TNCs).

In each sector now, the biggest multinational corporations have been forced to recognise that it is clearance from citizens, not just from governments, that is necessary for democratic functioning. Coca-Cola was delivered that message in Plachimada in Kerala. Monsanto receives that message each time it tries to manipulate the Indian government into pushing its GMO seeds and patents on life.

Whether it is fisheries or aquaculture; toxic plants or toxic imports; land grab for factories; or real estate, free trade and the entry of TNCs, which threaten people's livelihoods, resources and health, local communities and grassroots movements are resisting. As their resistance resonates in village after village, from one investment site to another, a new environmental philosophy, based on the democratic decentralisation of control over natural resource, is emerging. Pressure from people is forcing the government to recall its role as protector of public interest and the country's natural and cultural heritage. Localisation is emerging as an antidote to globalisation, and to unrestrained commercial greed. It is reasserting itself as the democratic option of the future.

In 2016, I was invited to Barcelona, Spain, to participate in an initiative called Fearless Cities. The invitation said:

> In a world in which inequalities, xenophobia and authoritarianism are on the rise, towns and cities are standing up to defend human rights, democracy and the common good. Democracy was born at the local level, and that's where we can take it back, this time as part of an international network of refuge, solidarity and hope.

This is how the planetary freedom movement is evolving and will grow—from the bottom up, decentralised, self-organised, and interconnected.

As millions are uprooted and become refugees, they seek shelter in other places. The refugee crisis is being use to polarise society based on a politics of hate. It is only the deep consciousness of being earth citizens that becomes a source of love in times of pervasive hate, of interconnectedness in times of violent separations and divisions, of hope in times of hopelessness, of creative and compassionate ways of dealing with refugees.

The dualisms created by the mechanical mind prevent us from imagining that we can be both local, rooted in a place, and planetary in our consciousness; that we can be distinctive, and unique individuals while we are part of one humanity; that global integration does not have to be vertical, with the 1% extracting life and freedom from nature and society and crushing those who support them, but the planetary and horizontal unity of consciousness and compassion, of interconnectedness and interbeing. Gandhi imagined it as an 'ever expanding, never ascending oceanic circle':

> Life will not be a pyramid with the apex sustained by the bottom. But it will be an oceanic circle whose centre will be the individual always ready to perish for the circle of villages, till at last the whole becomes one life composed of individuals, never aggressive in their arrogance but ever humble, sharing the majesty of the oceanic circle of which they are integral units. Therefore, the outermost circumference will not wield power to crush the inner circle, but will give strength to all within and will derive its own strength from it.[1]

Swadeshi—the resurgence of real wealth, real work and well-being

'Swadeshi' is the Indian word for local living economies, for economic sovereignty and economic democracy. Swadeshi is based on local economies that grow into national economies, and finally into a planetary economy, in alignment with nature and people's real freedoms, real wealth creation, and well-being at every level. Creating economies that work for the 99%, not just the 1%, is an ethical, ecological, economic and human imperative.

Self-reliance was an important aspect of the swadeshi movement in India. It was both the commitment to produce what we need and to buy only Indian products, as well as a boycott of British clothing.

The big shift taking place around the world is from the structural violence of the money machine to non-violent economies, from forced globalisation degrading the environment, to localisation through which we become co-creators with the earth to produce more and better food, clothing, shelter, and mobility for all. Initiatives in ecological economies, the transition movement and local currencies, and economies for the common good, are all striving towards the resurgence of real economies that increase real wealth defined as well-being.

The resurgence of real wealth must be based on the recovery of the commons, and on the creation of new commons that are beyond the reach of global corporations and the centralising, privatising corporate states. Twenty years of corporate globalisation, based on the WTO rules written by the Toxic Cartel and the Agribusiness Cartel, combined with five decades of a Toxic Cartel-driven non-Green Revolution, have pushed Indian farmers to the brink.

Instead of revisiting the unfair rules of globalisation and trade liberalisation, the corporations that created the distress are trying to turn the crisis into an opportunity to expand their profits and control. They want long distance trade and contract farming to lock every farmer into slavery. They seek to intensify industrial farming and its monocultures. They are proposing 'one agriculture, one market', a slogan embodying monocultures and monopolies that governments are picking up as the new 'development'.

Gandhi defined swadeshi as the 'spirit in us which restricts us to the use and services of our immediate surroundings to the exclusion of the more remote'. Localisation is an ethical and ecological imperative. It reduces our ecological footprint while opening opportunities for creative, meaningful work, producing quality, and enhancing well-being. It fixes the broken circle between production and consumption. The current system is based on the separation of the producer and consumer, with producers and the earth being exploited, and consumers being driven by thoughtless consumerism, based on the illusion of 'cheap'. Globally traded and industrially produced and distributed food and clothing appear cheap because the costs to society and the planet are not taken into account. 'Consumerism' is the social addiction to junk which keeps the money machine running. True costs show that the ecological, the local, the fossil free non-industrial systems work better for the planet, for producers and consumers.

The 'cheap' of a corporate-driven globalised economy is extremely costly, when true cost accounting is done. We have calculated $1.3 billion as the true social and ecological cost of chemical farming in India, annually.[2] If the deaths of Indian farmers growing Bt cotton and the deaths of women workers in Bangladesh's garment factories were internalised in the costs of what we wear, no one could afford the 'cheap' clothing of the big chains. If the destruction of small farms, the uprooting and displacement of farming communities, the desertification of soil, the disappearance of biodiversity, the torture of animals in factory farms, the destabilisation of the climate, the disease epidemics were internalised in the cost of what we eat, the 'cheap' food, grown with Monsanto's chemicals and GMOs, traded by Cargill, retailed by Walmart and Amazon, processed by Nestlé and Pepsi, would be unaffordable. If feeding the world was the goal, these corporations would not need to make local, sustainable alternatives illegal.

As Schumacher, the author of *Small is Beautiful*[3] and *Buddhist Economics* points out, simplicity and non-violence are the basis of an economy of well-being, and such an economy must be localised:

> From the point of view of Buddhist economics…production from local resources for local needs is the most rational way of economic life, while dependence on imports from afar and the consequent need to produce for export to unknown and distant peoples is highly uneconomic and justifiable only in exceptional cases and on a small scale.[4]

New forms of totalitarian control are being created through new methods of extracting superprofits from society, new convergences of technologies and new concentrations of power. The guiding principle of corporate globalisation is centralised, industrialised, and mechanised modes of production. Gandhi turned this principle on its head and envisioned a decentralised, homegrown, hand-crafted mode of production. In his words, 'Not mass production, but production by the masses.'

I have never thought the word 'protectionism' as negative. Protecting the earth, our homes, our families, our cultures is a duty that is vital to sustain our lives, ecologically and socially. Swadeshi, or economic democracy based on local economies, is also necessary to prevent the rise of xenophopia and hate in this age of discontent with dominant systems. While an anti-globalisation and anti-immigrant rhetoric dominated the Brexit vote and the US presidential election in 2016, it went hand in hand with further integration of the global financial system and a politics of hate. Worse, while keeping people divided, it institutionalised more deeply the rule of the 1% and immunity for the billionaires. People voted for change, they got more of the same.

In earth democracy, no species and no culture is expendable.

How the 1% Subverts Democracy

Diversity ensures balance; balance ensures that no single species, no one culture dominates the rest. That is why real democracy, diversity and decentralisation go hand in hand.

Gandhi's notion of swaraj simultaneously indicates a path to freedom from the Empire as well as a path to freedom from hate:

> To reject foreign manufactures merely because they are foreign, and to go on wasting national time and money in the promotion, in one's country, of manufactures for which it is not suited, would be criminal folly, and a negation of the swadeshi spirit. A true votary of swadeshi will never harbour ill-will towards the foreigner; he will not be actuated by antagonism towards anybody on earth. Swadeshism is not a cult of hatred. It is a doctrine of selfless service that has its roots in the purest ahimsa, i.e. love.
>
> If we follow the swadeshi doctrine, it would be your duty and mine to find out neighbours who can supply our wants and to teach them to supply them where they do not know how to proceed, assuming that there are neighbours who are in want of healthy occupation. Then every village in India will almost be a self-supporting and self-contained unit, exchanging only such necessary commodities with other villages where they are not locally producible. In such an economic system there will be an organic relationship between production, distribution and consumption.[5]

Satyagraha: the resurgence of real resistence, real democracy

Satyagraha, or the force of truth, was Gandhi's word for non-cooperation with and non-participation in systems, structures, laws, paradigms, and policies that destroy the earth and rob us of our humanity and our freedoms. Satyagraha is the deepest practice of democracy, a 'No' from the highest consciousness, the moral duty to not cooperate with unjust and brute law and exploitative and undemocratic processes. Higher moral laws compel citizens to disobey lower laws that institutionalise injustice and violence. Thoreau puts it succinctly:

> The only obligation which I have a right to assume is to do at any time what I think is right. It is truly enough said that a corporation has no conscience; but a corporation of conscientious men is a corporation with a conscience. Law never made men a whit more just; and, by means of their respect for it, even the well-disposed are daily made the agents of injustice.

I would add that as long as the superstition exists that the fictions and illusions of the 1% must be believed in, and be allowed to destroy real knowledge, real intelligence, real wealth, and real freedom, our slavery to the 1% will persist. As slaves to the edifice of illusions that creates the mechanical mind and the money machine, we become complicit in the processes that are destroying the earth and humanity.

But satyagraha, or non-cooperation, passive resistance, did not begin with Gandhi or Thoreau. It has been the deepest democratic practice through the ages to defend freedom. Gandhi himself acknowledged that he did not 'invent' satyagraha, he learnt it from the people of India. As he writes in *Hind Swaraj*:

> The fact is that, in India, the nation at large has generally used passive resistance in all departments of life. We cease to cooperate with our rulers when they displease us. This is passive resistance.[6]

Satyagraha is more important than ever today, in our age of 'post truth'. It was, and has always been, about awakening our conscience, our inner power, to resist an externally imposed cruel and unjust system.

How the 1% Subverts Democracy

Gandhi's Salt Satyagraha inspired Navdanya's Seed Satyagraha, or the Seed Freedom movement. Since 1987, when I first heard corporations talking about owning seeds through Intellectual Property Rights (IPR), my conscience refused to accept it. I made a lifetime commitment to saving seeds, to not cooperate with IPR systems that make seed saving and seed exchange a crime.

Bija Satyagraha (Seed Satyagraha) is a people's movement for the resurgence of the real seed, of the intelligence of farmers to be breeders, and to co-evolve with the intelligence of the seed towards diversity resilience and quality. TheBija Satyagraha pledge that our farmers take says,

> We have received these seeds from nature and our ancestors. It is our duty to future generations to hand them over in the richness of diversity and integrity in which we received them. Therefore, we will not obey any law, or adopt any technology that interferes in our higher duties to the earth and the future generations. We will continue to save and share our seeds.

Since 1991, Navdanya has organised farmers through the Bija Satyagraha movement to keep seed in farmer's hands and not cooperate with IPR laws and seed acts that are based on the illusion that seeds are inventions of corporations like Monsanto. In 1993, half-a-million farmers participated in a historic Bija Satyagraha rally at Bangalore's Cubbon Park, the first international protest against General Agreement on Tariffs and Trade (GATT)/WTO.

In 2014, through the Seed Satyagraha we stopped a seed law that would have made farmers saving and exchanging their local varieties, illegal. The Global Seed Freedom Movement practiced similar satyagrahas in Europe, Colombia, and California to prevent the introduction of compulsory registration laws that criminalise farmers' seed varieties.

The Jal Satyagraha against Coca-Cola in Kerala and in Doon Valley stopped the beverage giant from stealing water. The Water Democracy movement to defend the Ganga and prevent privatisation of its water for Delhi halted the World Bank-funded water privatisation project. Satyagrahas initiated by women against industrial aquaculture in Tamil Nadu, Andhra Pradesh and Odisha successfully protected people's right to safe drinking water.

Real freedom is based on the freedom to defend our rivers and our water as a commons; to defend our seeds, and our healthy, nutritious indigenous foods.

We undertook the Sarson Satyagraha (Mustard Satyagraha) in 1998 against the ban on indigenous cold pressed edible oils to facilitate the dumping of GMO soya oil in India. That is why cold pressed oils, including mustard oil, are available in the country today. In 2015, we renewed the Sarson Satyagraha when an attempt was made to introduce GMO mustard. In December 2015, we undertook a satyagraha when pseudo safety laws were trying to shut down Gandhi's cold press oil mill in Sevagram, Maharashtra. These satyagrahas have brought the right to safe, healthy indigenous food centre stage.

In 1998, the global soya lobby started to dump GMO soya oil in India and manipulated a ban on indigenous cold press oil mills as a result of which 5,00,000 village oil mills across the country were closed. No indigenous oils were available. Members of the Women's Food Sovereignty Alliance called me from the slums of Delhi and said we must bring our mustard oil back. That is when we started the Sarson Satyagraha, civil disobedience against the laws that banned our mustard, and the making of our own edible oils, from our own oilseeds, with our own hands.

In 2017, a satyagraha organised by the Mahila Anna Swaraj (Food Sovereignty in Women's Hand), a network of more than five million women producers, was successful in blocking food safety standards that would have shut down women's artisanal processing. And satyagrahas of the tribals in Niyamgiri in Odisha and of peasants in Singur and Nandigram in West Bengal halted the corporate land grab unleashed by globalisation.

Examples of trying to make the local, ecological and democratic alternatives illegal include repeated attempts by seed corporations to criminalise local seeds and seed-saving by farmers, and the move to make local, artisanal food production illegal.[7]

Fresh, local and artisanal food, without chemical additives and industrial processing, is recognised as the healthiest food. This is why, until the 1990s, food processing in India was reserved for the small-scale and cottage industry sector. The WTO rules changed our food and agriculture systems dramatically. Today, we are living with food imperialism. We have become a sick nation due to the rapid spread of industrially-processed and junk foods.

The oils most Indians consume as 'vegetable oil' these days are industrially processed, imported palm and soya oils. Unlike sesame, mustard, groundnut, linseed and coconut, these are not true oils because they cannot be processed in *ghanis* or through cold press.

The oil from soya is extracted at high temperatures in hexane solvent extraction plants. Hexane is a crude oil-based organic solvent with many industrial uses and is a neurotoxicant. No tests or labelling inform citizens about this process and the inclusion of GMOs in our food chain. In industrially refined oils, 30 per cent 'blending' in 'refined' oils is legal. The adulterants are labelled as 'vegetable oils', without letting consumers know that vegetable oils include oil from the toxic GMO cotton seed. GMO foods are not allowed in India, yet Bt cotton seed oil is being freely blended in industrial 'edible' oils.

It is industrial food with added chemicals that needs to be tested in labs, not just for artificial ingredients but also for the impact of chemical additives and industrial processing on our health. The new food safety rules are arbitrary because they do not differentiate between artisanal, chemical-free processing of oil from the industrial, chemical, crude oil-based processes. Imposing chemical labs on a *ghani* ensures that safe foods made in the artisanal sector are shut down in order to create a monopoly by corporations for unhealthy and unsafe foods.

Pure virgin oil from the *ghani* is still sold at Gandhi's Sevagram Ashram and people come from far and wide to buy it. Food safety in the artisanal sector needs participatory systems where citizens who produce the oil and those who consume it set the standards of quality and reliability. Just as there are participatory guarantee systems for organic production, we need participatory systems for artisanal food processing.

Imported and adulterated edible oils dominate the market because they are subsidised and their ecological and health costs are hidden and externalised. For instance, in India, the import duty of edible oil was reduced in 1998 from 300 per cent to zero, an indirect subsidy. In addition, the Indian government subsidises soya oil by Rs 15 per litre.[8] This is over and above the subsidy given by the US government to it.

The expansion of palm oil plantations is the primary reason for the destruction of rainforests in Indonesia; the expansion of

How the 1% Subverts Democracy

GMO soya plantations is a major cause for the destruction of the Amazon rainforests and Cerrado, in Brazil and Argentina. Forest destruction contributes 18 per cent of greenhouse gases and 85 per cent of rainforest destruction is accounted for by the expansion of industrial agriculture. Palm oil cultivation in Indonesia accounted for an estimated two to nine per cent of all tropical land use emissions from 2000 to 2010. The country was the world's seventh-largest polluter in 2009, and deforestation accounted for about 30 per cent of these emissions, ranking second (behind Brazil) in pollution due to deforestation. Soya cultivation in India destroys soil fertility and is ruining farmers in Madhya Pradesh and Maharashtra. Gandhi's *ghani* is a symbol of our freedom from a new corporate imperialism trying to control what we grow on our farms, how we process our food and what we eat. While the current food safety laws originate in the Sanitary and Phytosanitary Agreement of the WTO, with the Doha Round of the WTO as good as dead after the Nairobi Ministerial held from December 15-19, 2015, the toxic food industry is getting ready to impose the Trans-Pacific Partnership trade deal which will fully dismantle our food safety systems. We must act now to reclaim our right to grow and eat safe, healthy, indigenous foods.

On January 30, 2016, Gandhi's martyrdom day, I joined Gandhians in Sevagram, in defence of Gandhi's *ghani* as a symbol of swadeshi food. And we have made a commitment to introduce tiny *ghanis* in as many villages as possible, to create artisanal livelihoods, to make healthy cold press oil accessible to all, and to create a local circular economy so that farmers can grow the diversity of oilseeds that have been displaced by imports of bad oil, and by the spread of monocultures.

In April 2017, on the anniversary of the Champaran

Satyagraha, we undertook a satyagraha yatra, starting in Meerut. We visited Varanasi to celebrate the 1810 movement against the British imposed house tax. On April 17, we undertook a pilgrimage to Champaran, the day Gandhi started his satyagraha against the forced cultivation of indigo. We then joined the valiant communities of Singur and Nandigram who prevented a land grab for an industrial project through a land satyagraha. After paying homage to those who participated in the Salt Satyagraha of 1930 by travelling the salt road in Odisha, we concluded our yatra on Earth Day at the Navdanya community seed bank in Odisha, which has spread seeds of hope across India, after cyclones, after the tsunami and after repeated droughts.

Over four-and-a-half decades, I have participated in many satyagrahas, beginning with the Chipko movement, and my commitment to our common freedoms grows deeper with time. The planetary satyagraha we need today is for each of us to break free of the prisons in our minds created by the 1% through constructs and illusions, while we unleash our intelligence and latent power to begin a resurgence of the real. Today's non-cooperation movement begins with not subscribing to the fictions and falsehoods through which we are colonised, and by not cooperating with the structures of violence and domination built through these fictions to uphold structures of extraction and exploitation. Breaking free of the 1% is the satyagraha of our times.

Real freedom and real wealth creation call for the practice of satyagraha, swaraj and swadeshi with integrity and integration. Resistance without another imagination rooted in the real, combined with constructive action, will not create another world. Sowing the seeds of freedom is not imaginary; it is a conscious act, an act in which we become one with the earth. Oneness is our being, our source of power. Our power to resist, non-violently. Our power to co-create, non-violently.

Recently, the High Court of Uttarakhand in India ruled that Himalayan mountain ranges, glaciers, rivers, streams, rivulets, lakes, jungles, the air, forests, meadows, dales, wetlands, grasslands and springs are living beings and legal entities with rights.[9] The legislature in Madhya Pradesh recognised the personhood of the Narmada river in May 2017 to ensure 'conservation of aquatic biodiversity'. These juridical and paradigm shifts that are taking place create new possibilities for sustainable societies and earth democracies. The Monsanto Tribunal and General Assembly that we organised in October 2016 in The Hague had brought witnesses from across the world on one platform to share evidence on Monsanto's crimes against nature and humanity on record. This is earth democracy in practice. And while we resist the untruth, the violent, we are also sowing seeds of hope and freedom.

Seeding the future, seeding freedom through earth democracy

Seeding the future when possible extinction stares us in the face, seeding freedom when all freedoms of all beings are being closed for the limitless freedom of the 1% to exploit the earth and people, to manipulate life and our minds, calls for a quantum leap in our imaginations, our intelligences, our capacity for compassion and love, as well as our courage for creative nonviolent resistance and non-cooperation with a system that is driving us to extinction.

Our only option is to heal the earth, and in so doing, heal

and reclaim our humanity, creating hope for our only future—as one humanity on one planet. Stephen Hawking's two options—become extinct or escape from planet earth to other planets, are not the only two futures available to humanity.[10]

There is a third option beyond extinction and escape, the alternative of rejuvenating the earth to be able to continue to live here, in the particular places and the planet we call home. This is our evolutionary challenge. If we awaken to our own intelligence and evolutionary potential, and the intelligence pervading our planet and the universe we do not need to slip into the despair and hopelessness of inevitable extinction, or the hubris of conquest and mastery over other planets.

Elon Musk wants to create a Space X city on Mars: 'By talking about the Space X Mars architecture, I want to make Mars seem possible—make it seem as though it is something that we can do in our lifetime,' he writes, adding, 'There really is a way that anyone could go if they wanted to.' Musk believes the threshold for a self-sustaining city on Mars would be one million people. Current calculations indicate that it would take between 40 to 100 years 'to achieve a fully self-sustaining civilization on Mars.'[11]

In less than the one hundred years that the masters of the universe would like one-eighth of the human population to climb into a spaceship and escape to Mars (there is, of course, no mention of the rest of humanity and the rest of species) humanity could regenerate the planet, rejuvenate the earth's soils, water, biodiversity, bring about a balance between humans, and provide enough food for all.

For Musk, as for Hawking, there are only two fundamental paths for mankind—that we stay on earth forever, eventually succumbing to an extinction event, or to become a 'space bearing-civilization and a multi-planetary species'. Musk, like all men suffering from technological hubris, does not seem to understand that being a planetary citizen does not need space travel. It means being concious that we are part of the universe and the earth, and that we need to live in accordance with the laws of the universe, of the earth. The most fundamental law is to recognise that we share the planet with other beings, and that we have a duty to care for our common home.

The physical capacity to organise space flights has already been achieved. We now need to evolve our planetary consciousness as earth citizens. The wider our consciousness, the smaller our ecological footprint. I would translate for the contemporary evolutionary moment Gandhi's distillation of universal ecological responsibility when he said, 'The earth provides enough for everyone's needs, but not for a few people's greed.' Today, we need to recognise that the earth provides enough for all beings and their future evolution. Extinction looks inevitable only in a worldview driven by greed, by hubris, by a mechanical, militarised intelligence for conquest. To assume that flying to Mars is equal to creating life on Mars, and building a self-sustaining civilisation there is the leap of hubris and arrogance, ignorance and indifference.

Both Hawking and Musk seem to have ignored the fact that the earth is a self-organised, living planet which creates the conditions for its life and all the species that have evolved on it. That the earth, and every living being, the tiniest of cells, has the capacity to heal, renew, regenerate. Hope comes from this potential, from the fact that we share the planet with millions of species. It is irresponsible, immoral, and unethical to think that we can continue to trash the planet and escape to another one, even if it were to become technologically feasible to do so.

Staying home is an ecological imperative, an ethical imperative.

It is also a joyful option. It is the practice of Oikonomia as the art of living. It is earth democracy in action, cultivating and expanding the freedoms of all beings.

In the face of the hyper anthropocentrism and hyper greed of the 1%, which is exterminating the diversity of species, and rendering the 99% disposable, our power for change comes from being part of the earth family. In the awareness that we are one with the earth and all her beings we become aware that we are one as humanity. The web of life unites us. The power of Big Money and its political machine divides us by locking us in narrow, fragmented, constructed identities, creating the illusion of our separation from the earth, and through that separation, the illusion that it is the money machine that runs our lives. That we will have no food without the Monsantos and Cargills, no water without the Cokes and the Pepsis, no health without Big Pharma, no friends without Facebook, no communication without Twitter, no money without Big Banks, no energy without Big Oil, no knowledge without Big Data.

A mechanical mind locks us into thinking that every inclusion of the Other in our being and consciousness is a shrinking of our space and our freedoms. But the ecological space, where life renews and regenerates, is not a two-dimensional Cartesian space. It is a four-dimensional space of 'desha' and 'kala', space and time, where life evolves in intelligence and vibrance and diversity. The greater the density of interactions and relations in life's ecological space, the more we enlarge our own freedoms and possibilities.

The business of grabbing and money-making, through a violent extractive economy that the 1% have built is burdening the earth and humanity with unbearable and non-sustainable costs, and has brought us to the brink of extinction.

How the 1% Subverts Democracy

We do not have to escape from the earth, we have to escape from the illusions that enslave our minds and make extinction look inevitable

We are living through the latest phase of an epic struggle that has shaped human history through the ages, between the power of domination and destruction, mastery and ownership, and the non-violent power of co-creation, cooperation, co-evolution. The power of violence and destruction comes from separation—from nature and from each other. Our non-violent power comes from interconnectedness and oneness. This is why seed by seed, farmer by farmer, plate by plate, we are sowing an alternative based on intelligence and science, responsibility and awareness, care and compassion. And in the process, more species are flourishing, there is more food, more rejuvenation of our biodiversity, our soil, and our water. The potential for a healthier planet and society, with more knowledge among more people, and an earth democracy based on the intelligence of all life evolving is before us, and it is real. It heralds the resurgence of the real.

Endnotes

[1] M.K. Gandhi, *Panchayat Raj*. Ahmedabad: Navajivan, 1996, pp. 11-12.
[2] Vandana Shiva and Vaibhav Singh, *Wealth per Acre*. New Delhi: Natraj Publishers, 2015.
[3] Ernst F. Schumacher, *Small Is Beautiful: Economics As If People Mattered*, first published in 1973; New York: Harper & Row.
[4] Maria Popova, 'Buddhist Economics: How to Start Prioritizing People Over Products and Creativity Over Consumption', *Brainpickings.org*. https://www.brainpickings.org/2014/07/07/buddhist-economics-schumacher/.
[5] R.K. Prabhu and V.R. Rao (Ed.) *From the Mind of Mahatma Gandhi*. Ahmedabad: Navajivan, 1966, Chapter 87. http://www.mkgandhi.org/ebks/mindofmahatmagandhi.pdf.

[6] MK Gandhi, *Hind Swaraj.* Ahmedabad: Navajivan, 1996, p. 58.

[7] 'Seed Satyagraha (Civil Disobedience To End Seed Slavery)', *Seedsfreedom.info.* https://Seedfreedom.Info/Campaign/Seed-Satyagraha-Civil-Disobedience-To-End-Seed-Slavery/. Published on September 8, 2015.

[8] 'Govt to introduce edible oil in PDS channel from June', *The Economic Times.* https://economictimes.indiatimes.com/news/economy/policy/govt-to-introduce-edible-oil-in-pds-channel-from-june/articleshow/2999261.cms. Published on April 30, 2008. See also, Ramesh Chand, 'Need to evaluate free edible oil import', *Business Standard.* https://www.business-standard.com/article/opinion/need-to-evaluate-free-edible-oil-import-118052900002_1.html. Published on May 29, 2018; and Anindita Dey, 'Food ministry seeks pulses, edible oil subsidy extension', *Business Standard.* https://www.business-standard.com/article/markets/food-ministry-seeks-pulses-edible-oil-subsidy-extension-111022500028_1.html. Published on January 20, 2013.

[9] 'Uttarakhand HC Declares Air, Glaciers, Forests, Springs, Waterfalls etc. as Legal Persons [Read Judgment]', *Livelaw News Network.* http://www.livelaw.in/uttarakhand-hc-declares-air-glaciers-forests-springs-waterfalls-etc-legal-persons/. Published on April 1, 2017.

[10] Chris McDermott, 'Stephen Hawking: We Have 100 Years to Find a New Planet', *Eco Watch.* http://www.ecowatch.com/stephen-hawking-bbc-2392439489.html. Published on May 4, 2017; Sarah Knapton, 'Tomorrow's World Returns To BBC with Startling Warning from Stephen Hawking–We Must Leave Earth', *The Telegraph.* http://www.telegraph.co.uk/science/2017/05/02/tomorrows-world-returns-bbc-startling-warning-stephen-hawking/. Published on May 2, 2017.

[11] Hannah Osborne, 'Elon Musk Reveals Vision for a SpaceX City on Mars', *Newsweek.* http://www.newsweek.com/elon-musk-mars-spacex-martian-city-625994. Published on June 15, 2017.

Epilogue

In March 2015, Bill Gates showed an image of the coronavirus during a TED Talk and told the audience that it was what the greatest catastrophe of our time would look like. The real threat to life, he said, is 'not missiles, but microbes.'[1] When the coronavirus pandemic swept over the earth like a tsunami five years later, he revived the war language, describing the pandemic as 'a world war'.

'The coronavirus pandemic pits all of humanity against the virus,' he said.[2]

In fact, the pandemic is not a war. The pandemic is a *consequence* of war. A war against life. The mechanical mind connected to the money machine of extraction has created the illusion of humans as separate from nature, and nature as dead, inert raw material to be exploited. But, in fact, we are part of the biome. And we are part of the virome. The biome and the virome are us. When we wage war on the biodiversity of our forests, our farms, and in our guts, we wage war on ourselves.

The health emergency of the coronavirus is inseparable from the health emergency of extinction, the health emergency of biodiversity loss, and the health emergency of the climate crisis. All of these emergencies are rooted in a mechanistic, militaristic, anthropocentric worldview that considers humans separate from—and superior to—other beings. Beings we can own, manipulate, and control. All of these emergencies are rooted in an economic model based on the illusion of limitless growth and limitless greed, which violate planetary boundaries, and destroy the integrity of ecosystems and individual species.

New diseases arise because a globalized, industrialized, inefficient agriculture invades habitats, destroys ecosystems, and manipulates animals, plants, and other organisms with no respect for their integrity or their health. We are linked worldwide through the spread of diseases like the coronavirus because we have invaded the homes of other species, manipulated plants and animals for commercial profits and greed, and cultivated monocultures. As we clear-cut forests, as we turn farms into industrial monocultures that produce toxic, nutritionally empty commodities, as our diets become degraded through industrial processing with synthetic chemicals and genetic engineering, and as we perpetuate the illusion that earth and life are raw materials to be exploited for profits, we are indeed connecting. But instead of connecting on a continuum of health by protecting biodiversity, integrity, and self-organization of all living beings, including humans, we are connected through disease.

According to the International Labour Organization, '1.6 billion informal economy workers (representing the most vulnerable in the labour market), out of a worldwide total of two billion and a global workforce of 3.3 billion, have suffered massive damage to their capacity to earn a living. This is due to lockdown measures and/or because they work in the hardest-hit sectors.'[3] According to the World Food Programme, a quarter of a billion additional people will be pushed to hunger and 300,000 could die every day.[4] These, too, are pandemics that are killing people. Killing cannot be a prescription for saving lives.

Health is about life and living systems. There is no 'life' in the paradigm of health that Bill Gates and his ilk are promoting and imposing on the entire world. Gates has created global alliances to impose top-down analysis and prescriptions for health problems. He gives money to define the problems, and then he uses his influence and money to impose the solutions. And in the process, he gets richer. His 'funding' results in an erasure of democracy and biodiversity, of nature and culture. His 'philanthropy' is not just philanthrocapitalism. It is philanthroimperialism.

The coronavirus pandemic and lockdown have revealed even more clearly how we are being reduced to objects to be controlled, with our bodies and minds as the new colonies to be invaded. Empires create colonies, colonies enclose the commons of the indigenous living communities and turn them into sources of raw material to be extracted for profits. This linear, extractive logic is unable to see the intimate relations that sustain life in the natural world. It is blind to diversity, cycles of renewal, values of giving and sharing, and the power and potential of self-organising and mutuality. It is blind to the waste it creates and to the violence it unleashes. The extended coronavirus lockdown has been a lab experiment for a future without humanity.

On March 26, 2020, at a peak of the coronavirus pandemic and in the midst of the lockdown, Microsoft was granted a patent by the World Intellectual Property Organization (WIPO). Patent WO 060606 declares that 'Human Body Activity associated with a task provided to a user may be used in a mining process of a cryptocurrency system....'

The 'body activity' that Microsoft wants to mine includes radiation emitted from the human body, brain activities, body fluid flow, blood flow, organ activity, body movement such as eye movement, facial movement, and muscle movement, as well as any other activities that can be sensed and represented by images, waves, signals, texts, numbers, degrees, or any other information or data.

The patent is an intellectual property claim over our bodies and minds. In colonialism, colonisers assign themselves the right to take the land and resources of indigenous people, extinguish their cultures and sovereignty, and in extreme cases exterminate them. Patent WO 060606 is a declaration by Microsoft that our bodies and minds are its new colonies. We are mines of 'raw material'—the data extracted from our bodies. Rather than sovereign, spiritual, conscious, intelligent beings making decisions and choices with wisdom and ethical values about the impacts of our actions on the natural and social world of which we are a part, and to which we are inextricably related, we are 'users.' A 'user' is a consumer without choice in the digital empire.

But that's not the totality of Gates' vision. In fact, it is even more sinister—to colonise the minds, bodies, and spirits of our children before they even have the opportunity to understand what freedom and sovereignty look and feel like, beginning with the most vulnerable.

In May 2020, Governor Andrew Cuomo of New York announced a partnership with the Gates Foundation to 'reinvent education.' Cuomo called Gates a visionary and argued that the pandemic has created 'a moment in history when we can actually incorporate and advance [Gates'] ideas...all these buildings, all these physical classrooms—why with all the technology you have?'

In fact, Gates has been trying to dismantle the public education system of the United States for two decades. For him students are mines for data. That is why the indicators he promotes are attendance, college enrollment, and scores on a math and reading test, because these can be easily quantified and mined. In reimagining education, children will be monitored through surveillance systems to check if they are attentive while they are forced to take classes remotely, alone at home. The dystopia is one where children never return to schools, do not have a chance to play, do not have friends. It is a world without society, without relationships, without love and friendship.

How the 1% Subverts Democracy

As I look to the future in a world of Gates and Tech Barons, I see a humanity that is further polarized into large numbers of 'throw away' people who have no place in the new Empire. Those who are included in the new Empire will be little more than digital slaves.

Or, we can resist. We can seed another future, deepen our democracies, reclaim our commons, regenerate the earth as living members of a One Earth Family, rich in our diversity and freedom, one in our unity and interconnectedness. It is a healthier future. It is one we must fight for. It is one we must claim.

We stand at a precipice of extinction. Will we allow our humanity as living, conscious, intelligent, autonomous beings to be extinguished by a greed machine that does not know limits and is unable to put a break on its colonisation and destruction? Or will we stop the machine and defend our humanity, freedom, and autonomy to protect life on earth?

Endnotes

[1] Bill Gates, 'The Next Outbreak? We're Not Ready,' filmed March 2015 in Vancouver, B.C., TED video, 8:33, https://www.ted.com/talks/bill_gates_the_next_outbreak_we_re_not_ready.

[2] "'This Is Like a World War'": Bill Gates on Coronavirus,' *livemint*, last updated April 24, 2020, https://www.livemint.com/news/world/bill-gates-compares-fight-against-coronavirus-to-another-world-war-11587706313499.html.

[3] International Labour Organization News, 'ILO: As Job Losses Escalate, Nearly Half of Global Workforce at Risk of Losing Livelihoods,' press release, April 29, 2020, https://www.ilo.org/global/about-the-ilo/newsroom/news/WCMS_743036/lang--en/index.htm.

[4] David M. Beasley, 'Covid-19 Could Detonate a "Hunger Pandemic." With Millions at Risk, the World Must Act,' *Washington Post*, posted April 22, 2020, https://www.washingtonpost.com/opinions/2020/04/22/covid-19-could-detonate-hunger-pandemic-with-millions-risk-world-must-act.

Index

Index

Index

Index

Index

Index

191

Index